THE MAGIC OF MIXES

One quick look at your kitchen shelves
will tell you that mixes have become
a vital part of today's cooking. Our busy
lifestyles have created a major trend
toward the use of time-saving convenience
foods. Mixes are here to stay.

MIXES ARE EASY

With your own mixes you can
save almost three-fourths the time you
spend preparing most food items.

MIXES ARE ECONOMICAL

Although commercial mixes save time,
they don't save money. Save those extra
dollars by making mixes yourself.

MIXES ARE NUTRITIOUS

Meals from homemade mixes are fresher,
healthier, chockful of your own ingredients,
low in preservatives and additives.

MIXES ARE VERSATILE

The possibilities are endless.
A multipurpose mix such as QUICK MIX
makes dozens of different delicious recipes.
Some, like TACO SEASONING MIX,
complement specific recipes. Others, like
CHICKEN MIX, are meals in themselves.

Economical, healthy, simple and fun
to make—it's easy to see why mixes are
the popular choice of today's cook.

Bantam Cookbooks
Ask your bookseller for the books you have missed

MAKE-A-MIX COOKERY
HOW TO MAKE YOUR OWN MIXES

by Karine Eliason,
Nevada Harward and
Madeline Westover

*This low-priced Bantam Book
has been completely reset in a type face
designed for easy reading, and was printed
from new plates. It contains the complete
text of the original hard-cover edition.*
NOT ONE WORD HAS BEEN OMITTED.

MAKE-A-MIX COOKERY

*A Bantam Book / published by arrangement with
HP Books*

PRINTING HISTORY
*HP Books edition published March 1978
2nd printing . . . May 1978   3rd printing . . . June 1978
Bantam edition / November 1978*

ISBN 0-553-12611-3

Published simultaneously in the United States and Canada

PRINTED IN THE UNITED STATES OF AMERICA

0 9 8 7 6 5 4 3

CONTENTS

MAKE-A-MIX
COOKERY

Baking & Cooking with Mixes

THE MAGIC OF MIXES

One quick look at your cupboard shelves will tell you that mixes have become an essential part of today's cooking. Our busy lifestyle has created a major trend toward the use of time-saving convenience foods and mixes are the popular choice for many of our cooking needs. Because the time-consuming part of cooking is assembling supplies and equipment and measuring ingredients, it's easy to see why mixes are so valuable to every cook.

If you really want to enjoy the magic of mixes, consider how much time, money and nutritional value you can save by making your own mixes. You make just what you need whenever you have the time and you have all the convenience of mix cooking with all the taste and food value of cooking "from scratch." In less time than it would take you to go to the store to purchase a mix or product, you can make enough at home for many meals.

MIXES ARE EASY

With your own mixes, you can save almost three-fourths the time you spend preparing food items. This is possible because you prepare for several meals at one time. Whether your family has 2 or 22 members, you can make just the right amount for each meal. The results are better planned, more delicious and more nutritious even when time is at a minimum. Most recipes from mixes are so easy your children can learn to make them.

MIXES ARE ECONOMICAL

Although commercial mixes provide convenience, they are generally advertised as *time-savers* rather than *money-savers*. Their prices increase regularly with rising labor and packaging costs. Why not save those extra dollars by providing the labor and packaging

1

yourself? Compare the cost per cup of commercial mixes with homemade mixes and you'll discover your mixes cost less than half the price of store mixes. You can save even more by watching for specials on staple items such as flour, sugar and shortening.

MIXES ARE NUTRITIOUS

There's a special satisfaction in choosing your own ingredients to cook with, and knowing what is in your foods. If you want to reduce the amount of preservatives and additives you consume, making your own mixes is the way to start. Commercial mixes are, of necessity, prepared for a long shelf life. Food value decreases with time and it is impossible to know just how old a product is at the time you purchase it. Some packaged mixes may be over a year old.

When you make meals from your own mixes, you'll notice the fresher flavor. The mix recipes in this book contain ingredients chosen for their health value.

MIXES ARE VERSATILE

The variety and extent to which mixes can be used is almost limitless. Perhaps you prefer a multipurpose mix such as QUICK MIX, which makes dozens of different recipes. The taste of each will far surpass results from commercial mixes.

Keep some general mixes like GINGERBREAD MIX, MUFFIN MIX and GRANOLA MIX on hand to make an assortment of dishes in minutes. With BASIC COOKIE MIX, you can make 6 types of cookies in the time it used to take to make only one! Won't it be handy to have 10 rolls of MOIST PIE CRUST MIX ready when you are?

Main dishes come from mixes, too. Try MEAT SAUCE MIX, CHICKEN MIX or GARDEN VEGETABLE MIX, all of which you can make ahead and store in the freezer! Use them in a different dish each time!

Some mixes are seasonings to complement specific recipes. Make individual packets of TACO SEASONING MIX, SPAGHETTI SAUCE MIX, SEASONED BREADCRUMB MIX and the various salad and beverage mixes and you're ready for any occasion! You'll find they're better than those you can buy. Some are so special you can't even buy them in stores.

The Ingredients

When you're making your own mixes, you'll want to use the best ingredients you can get, because foods you prepare are only as good as their contents. Always use fresh, high-quality products.

It's important to know what each ingredient offers to a recipe. This gives you the confidence to guarantee success every time in the kitchen. Here are some tips to help you make mixes and meals everyone will remember.

FLOURS

All-purpose Flour is best in most dry mixes. It is a blend of hard and soft wheat flours. Bleached or unbleached flour can be used alternately, but unbleached flour has a higher nutritional value. As moisture varies in wheat flours, some yeast bread recipes indicate an approximate measurement. Always begin with a small amount of flour and add more until the desired texture is reached.

Whole-wheat Flour can be used interchangeably with all-purpose flour. Wheat grain flours retain their original vitamins, minerals, fats and other components.

Cake Flour is used in BASIC CAKE MIX because it is made of soft wheat and bakes to a finer texture.

FATS

Butter and Margarine are used interchangeably in most recipes. However, butter produces a somewhat different texture and flavor than margarine and should be used in those recipes where specified. Butter and margarine are both perishable and mixes containing either should be refrigerated.

Vegetable Oils are pressed from seeds, fruits and nuts. These are more versatile and easily available than other liquid fats.

Hydrogenated Vegetable Shortening is preferred in most recipes. Mixes containing vegetable shortening

5

may be covered and stored in a cool, dry place for 3 months or more.

EGGS

Fresh eggs are a boost to every recipe because they have a much better texture and taste than eggs that have been stored awhile. Use large eggs, about 2 ounces in weight.

LEAVENS

Active Dry Yeast is convenient for mixing purposes. Yeast is comprised of living organisms that feed on sugars and produce alcohol and carbon dioxide. Be certain the liquid you add yeast to is lukewarm, about 105° to 125°F (40° to 50°C).

Baking Powder generally starts to work when it is combined with liquid, but its principal impact on a product is increased when the product is heated. Double-acting baking powder is preferred for its availability and consistency.

Baking Soda alone has no leavening properties, but when used in combination with acid ingredients such as sour milk or molasses it produces a tender crumb texture.

SUGARS

Sugars contribute sweetness and tenderness to foods. In breads, sugar aids in producing a golden brown crust. Small pinches of sugar added to certain vegetables increases their flavor. Granulated sugar is usually used in these recipes. Powdered sugar, brown sugar, honey and molasses are specified. They are not interchangeable with granulated sugar.

SPICES

Sometimes the difference between an outstanding and a mediocre dish is the seasoning added. Our recipes allow you to use a wide variety of herbs, seasonings and spices. For best results, use recently purchased, high-quality spices because spices tend to lose their flavor in a short time.

VEGETABLES, MEATS & POULTRY

The greatest care should be used in preparing vegetables, meats and poultry for storage. It is essential to use fresh, clean, top-quality ingredients. Follow directions carefully for preparing, freezing and storing frozen mixes.

INSTANT NONFAT DRY MILK

With milk solids added to a dry mix, you have the option of adding water to the recipe instead of milk. Adding milk gives extra enrichment.

Equipment & Procedures

On the whole, Make-A-Mix Cookery is very similar to the way you cook now. You probably already have all the equipment you need for measuring, mixing and storing the ingredients.

The procedures for combining ingredients will be slightly different than cooking "from scratch." You will spend a little extra time preparing your mixes, but you'll save much more time in the final preparation of recipes. Make up several mixes at a time. Because you're working mainly with dry ingredients, the cleanup will be minimal. In just a short time, you can fill your shelves with an abundance of mixes that will make cooking more enjoyable for weeks to come.

MEASURING

Accuracy in measuring ingredients is necessary to insure satisfactory results in your cooking. You should have:

- A set of dry measuring cups
- A liquid measuring cup with pouring spout
- A set of measuring spoons
- A straight-edged spatula
- A rubber scraper

Dry Ingredients should be measured in a cup with a flush rim for leveling. Lightly spoon ingredients into the cup and level with a straight-edged spatula.

Liquid Ingredients require a transparent measuring cup with markings and a pouring spout. Measure liquid ingredients at eye-level.

Moist Ingredients such as brown sugar, soft breadcrumbs, grated cheese, coconut or raisins should be firmly packed so they hold the shape of the cup when turned out.

Solid Ingredients such as vegetable shortening should be pressed firmly into the measuring cup or spoon so no air pockets remain. Level with a straight-edged spat-

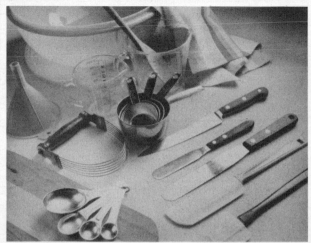

1/These basic kitchen utensils are all you need
for making mixes. A pastry blender makes it easier
to cut shortening into dry ingredients.

2/Lots of airtight canisters, jars and cans are
useful for storing mixes. Freezer containers
should allow for expansion of frozen mixes.

3/Store seasoning mixes in aluminum foil packets folded and wrapped tightly to keep out air.

4/On each mix container write the name of the mix and the date by which it should be used. If you wish, also record the amount of mix and recipe page number.

ula. Use a rubber scraper to get all the shortening out of the measure.

MIXING

A real convenience in preparing mixes is a heavy-duty mixer. A small electric mixer, sifter or pastry blender will produce the same results but require more effort. If you do not have a pastry blender, you can use 2 knives to evenly distribute dry ingredients and fats.

You will definitely need an extra-large mixing bowl to combine mixes. If you do not have a bowl large enough to hold about 35 cups (9 quarts) of mix, a round-bottom dishpan is an alternative.

For dry mixes, the usual procedure is to combine all dry ingredients until evenly distributed, then cut in vegetable shortening, butter or margarine until the mixture reaches an even consistency.

STORING

For maximum freshness, the best way to store your mixes is in airtight containers placed in a cool, dry and dark place. Mixes to be stored in the freezer must be put in containers allowing for at least ½-inch expansion. Lightweight plastic bags and cottage cheese cartons are not suitable for freezer use. Your frozen mixes should be thawed in the refrigerator or microwave oven, and used immediately after thawing.

You will want to consider two methods of storing dry mixes, depending on your needs:

Large Canister Storage lets you store your mixes in one or several large containers. This is especially useful for QUICK MIX, HOT ROLL MIX and other mixes that make a large number of recipes. You can use large coffee cans lined with heavy plastic bags, large screw-top jars or airtight plastic containers or canisters you have on hand.

Premeasured Storage keeps just the amount you'll use in a specific recipe, so you won't have to measure it later. This is a good way to store BASIC CAKE MIX, PANCAKE MIX and the meat and seasoning mixes.

You can use plastic containers such as margarine tubs, drink mix cans or shortening cans with lids. Or try potato chip canisters, glass jars or heavy-duty foil packets. Your storage equipment can be as creative as your imagination.

LABELING

Before you place a mix on the shelf or in the freezer, make sure it's properly labeled! Resist the urge to store a mix when you plan to label it later, because later the mixes may all look alike! On each container, write the name of the mix and the date by which it should be used. In most instances the mixes can be stored longer than the specified time, but at the risk of loss in flavor, texture and nutrients. You may also want to write down the amount of mix in each container, particularly if you have divided the mix into premeasured amounts. In this case, you may want to record the page number of the mix recipe too.

MASTER MIXES

Here they are—the roadmaps to all the recipes in this book. A casual glance will show you the wide variety of Master Mixes and the even wider variety of uses. QUICK MIX, for example, makes over 30 recipes! These mixes are your beginning to hundreds of breads, main dishes, appetizers, cookies and many types of desserts.

Basically, Master Mixes come in 3 types:

The Dry Mixes contain only dry ingredients and keep 6 to 8 months. Shake the mixes before you use them, as some ingredients may have settled during storage. Dry mixes include HOT ROLL MIX, PANCAKE MIX and PUDDING & PIE MIX.

The Semi-Dry Mixes contain vegetable shortening, butter or margarine. These generally stay fresh for 10 to 12 weeks. Try WHEAT MIX, BASIC CAKE MIX and GINGERBREAD MIX.

Freezer-Refrigerator Mixes are moist and require cold storage in appropriate containers. These keep well about 3 months. Keep a supply of BRAISED BEEF CUBE MIX, MEXICAN MEAT MIX and MOIST PIE CRUST MIX for tasty, quick meals.

Be certain you familiarize yourself with the different kinds of Master Mixes and the many potential uses for each. You may find yourself creating new recipes with them! We recommend you start with QUICK MIX because of its versatility. Make up at least one main dish mix, such as CHICKEN MIX or MEATBALL MIX. Choose other mixes according to your particular tastes. How about CORNMEAL MIX,

BROWNIE MIX or OATMEAL MIX? Never let your shelves be without an ample supply of mixes.

Take time this weekend to make up a collection of mixes and discover your favorites. For a grand start, use BASIC COOKIE MIX to make 10 types of cookies at one time. Your family and friends will let you know how glad they are about your MAKE-A-MIX COOKERY.

Quick Mix

The most versatile of all mixes!

8½ cups all-purpose flour
1 tablespoon baking powder
1 tablespoon salt
2 teaspoons cream of tartar
1 teaspoon baking soda
1½ cups instant nonfat dry milk
2¼ cups vegetable shortening

In a large bowl, sift together all dry ingredients. Blend well. With pastry blender, cut in shortening until evenly distributed. Mixture will resemble cornmeal in texture. Put in a large airtight container. Label. Store in a cool, dry place. Use within 10 to 12 weeks. Makes about 13 cups of QUICK MIX.

Variation

Use 4¼ cups all-purpose flour and 4¼ cups whole-wheat flour instead of 8½ cups all-purpose flour. Increase baking powder to 2 tablespoons.

QUICK MIX makes:

If you're using QUICK MIX or BASIC CAKE MIX in altitudes above 3500 feet, increase the flour about ½ cup for better results.

Hot Roll Mix

Fix this mix ahead and you're ready to roll!

20 cups (5 lbs.) all-
  purpose flour
1¼ cups sugar

4 teaspoons salt
1 cup instant nonfat
  dry milk

Combine all ingredients in a large bowl. Stir together to distribute evenly. Put in a large airtight container. Label. Store in a cool, dry place. Use within 6 to 8 months. Makes about 22 cups of HOT ROLL MIX.

HOT ROLL MIX makes:

Swedish Cinnamon
  Twists, page 70
Tatonuts, page 72
Cinnamon Rolls, page 73
Cream Cheese Swirls,
  page 74
Butterscotch Butter
  Balls, pages 76–77
Pluckit, page 78
Mary's Honey-Walnut
  Swirl, pages 81–83
Pan Rolls, page 94

Orange Butterflake Rolls,
  page 95
Crescent Rolls, pages
  94, 234
Homemade White Bread,
  page 97
Hi-Light Onion Bread,
  page 98
Good-For-You Bread,
  page 99
Big Soft Pretzels, pages
  102–104, 231

Cornmeal Mix

*So convenient—you only add egg
and milk to make cornbread.*

4 cups all-purpose flour
1 tablespoon salt
¾ cup sugar
¼ cup baking powder

1 cup vegetable
  shortening
4½ cups cornmeal

In a large bowl, combine flour, salt, sugar and baking powder. Stir to blend well. With a pastry blender, cut in shortening until evenly distributed. Add cornmeal and mix well. Put in a large airtight container. Label.

Store in a cool, dry place. Use within 10 to 12 weeks. Makes about 10½ cups of CORNMEAL MIX.

CORNMEAL MIX makes:

Cornmeal Muffins, pages 87–88, 242

Dixie Spoon Bread, pages 101, 242

Cornbread Topping for Tamale Pie, pages 151, 152–153

Muffin Mix

Make many tempting muffins from one mix!

8 cups all-purpose flour
⅔ cup sugar
⅓ cup baking powder
1 tablespoon salt
1 cup vegetable shortening

In a large bowl, combine flour, sugar, baking powder and salt. Mix well. With a pastry blender, cut shortening into dry ingredients until evenly distributed. Put in a large airtight container. Label. Store in a cool, dry place. Use within 10 to 12 weeks. Makes about 10 cups of MUFFIN MIX.

MUFFIN MIX makes:

Melt-In-Your-Mouth Muffins, pages 85–86

Apple Muffins, page 86

Molasses-Bran Muffins, page 87

Whole-Wheat Muffins, page 89

Cranberry Cakes, page 199

Oatmeal Mix

Start your day right with oatmeal.

3 cups all-purpose flour
3½ teaspoons baking powder
1½ teaspoons salt
½ cup granulated sugar
1 cup brown sugar
1½ cups vegetable shortening
3 cups rolled oats

In a large bowl, sift together flour, baking powder, salt and granulated sugar. Stir in brown sugar. Mix well. With a pastry blender, cut in shortening until evenly distributed. Stir in oats and mix well. Put in a large airtight container. Label. Store in a cool, dry place. Use within 10 to 12 weeks. Makes about 9 cups of OATMEAL MIX.

OATMEAL MIX makes:

Oatmeal Muffins, page 85
Oat Pancakes, page 91
Oatmeal Cookies, page
  174
Caramelita Oatmeal
  Bars, pages 186–187

Fruit Bar Cookies, page
  188
Peach Blossom Dessert,
  page 217

Pancake Mix

*If pancakes are popular at your house,
you'll appreciate this mix.*

10 cups all-purpose flour
2½ cups instant nonfat
  dry milk

½ cup sugar
¼ cup baking powder
2 tablespoons salt

Combine all ingredients in a large bowl. Stir together to blend well. Put in a large airtight container. Label. Store in a cool, dry place. Use within 6 to 8 months. Makes about 13 cups of PANCAKE MIX.

PANCAKE MIX makes:

Puff Oven Pancakes,
  page 89
Perfect Pancakes,
  page 90

Golden French Toast,
  page 92
Monte Cristo Sand-
  wiches, pages 126–128

Wheat Mix

Full of vitamins for delicious, mouth-watering meals.

6 cups whole-wheat flour
3 cups all-purpose flour
1½ cups instant nonfat
  dry milk
1 tablespoon salt
1 cup sugar
½ cup wheat germ
¼ cup baking powder
2 cups vegetable
  shortening

In a large bowl, combine whole-wheat flour, all-purpose flour, dry milk, salt, sugar, wheat germ and baking powder. Mix well. With a pastry blender, cut in shortening until evenly distributed. Put in a large airtight container. Label. Store in a cool, dry place. Use within 10 to 12 weeks. Makes about 14 cups of WHEAT MIX.

WHEAT MIX makes:

Quick Wheat Breakfast
  Cake, page 79
Quick Wheat Muffins,
  pages 88, 244
Favorite Wheat Pan-
  cakes, page 91
Wheat Waffles, page 91
Coffeetime Quick Bread,
  pages 99, 244

Braised Beef Cube Mix

Super stews begin with braised beef.

5 lbs. stew meat, cut in
  small chunks
1 (1⅜-oz.) pkg. onion
  soup mix
2 bay leaves
2 (10½-oz.) cans cream
  of mushroom soup
1 (10½-oz.) can golden
  mushroom soup
1 (10½-oz.) can cream
  of celery soup
1 qt. water

Preheat oven to 300°F (150°C). Combine all ingredients in a large covered casserole or Dutch oven. Stir until well-blended. Bake 3 to 4 hours until meat is tender. Cool. Put into eight 1-pint freezer containers, leaving ½-inch space at top. Seal and label containers. Freeze. Use within 3 months. Makes about 8 pints of BRAISED BEEF CUBE MIX.

BRAISED BEEF CUBE MIX makes:

Beef Bourguignonne, page 126

Western Beef Stew, page 146

Braised Beef Stroganoff, page 149

Or serve plain, or over hot cooked rice, mashed potatoes or buttered noodles.

Ready Hamburger Mix

The beginning of many meals, made in minutes.

4 lbs. lean ground beef	½ teaspoon pepper
1 large onion, chopped	½ teaspoon oregano
2 teaspoons salt	¼ teaspoon garlic salt

Brown ground beef in a heavy skillet. Drain. Add onion and continue cooking over medium-low heat until onions are golden. Add remaining ingredients. Cool. Spoon mixture into four 1-pint freezer containers, leaving ½-inch space at top. Seal and label containers. Freeze. Use within 3 months. Makes about 4 pints of READY HAMBURGER MIX.

READY HAMBURGER MIX makes:

Quick Taco Dip, page 112
Taco Salad, page 142
Spoon Tacos, page 143
Saturday Stroganoff, page 148
Enchilada Casserole, page 150

Spaghetti Casserole, page 154
Busy Day Casserole, page 154

Meat Sauce Mix

It's a lifesaver on those extra-busy days.

¼ cup vegetable
shortening
4 medium onions, sliced
3 cloves garlic, finely
chopped, or ⅜ tea-
spoon instant minced
garlic
2 cups finely chopped
celery
2 to 3 chopped carrots,
if desired

5 lbs lean ground beef
5 teaspoons salt
½ teaspoon pepper
3 tablespoons Worcester-
shire sauce
1 (14-oz.) bottle ketchup
1 (14-oz.) bottle "hot"
ketchup

Melt shortening in a large skillet over medium heat.
Add onions, garlic, celery and carrots, if desired. Sauté
until onions are golden. Add ground beef. Stir and
cook until meat is browned. Add salt, pepper, Worcestershire sauce, ketchup and "hot" ketchup. Cover and
simmer 20 minutes. Drain excess fat. Cool. Put into
five 1-pint freezer containers, leaving ½-inch space at
top. Cut through mixture with a knife several times
to remove air spaces. Seal and label containers. Freeze.
Use within 3 months. Makes about 5 pints of MEAT
SAUCE MIX.

MEAT SAUCE MIX makes:

Speedy Pizza, pages 125,
240
Rancher's Sloppy Joes,
pages 125, 240
Stuffed Hard Rolls,
page 135
Stuffed Green Peppers,
page 143
Hamburger Trio Skillet,
page 147

Hamburger-Noodle
Skillet, page 148
Layered Casserole Com-
plete, page 147
Chili Con Carne,
page 151
Tamale Pie, pages
151, 152–153
Or serve warm on ham-
burger buns.

How to Make Meat Sauce Mix

1/Sauté the onions, garlic and celery over medium heat until the onions are golden. Add ground beef.

2/Cook until the meat is browned, then add Worcestershire sauce, ketchup and "hot" ketchup.

Meatball Mix

Meatballs are always ready—
for appetizers, casseroles and main dishes.

4 lbs. lean ground beef	1 tablespoon salt
4 eggs, slightly beaten	2 tablespoons cornstarch
2 cups dry breadcrumbs	¼ teaspoon pepper
½ cup finely chopped onion	2 teaspoons Worcestershire sauce

Preheat oven to 400°F (205°C). Combine all ingredients in a large bowl. Blend well. Shape mixture into 1-inch balls. Place meatballs on ungreased baking sheets and bake 10 to 15 minutes, until browned. Remove immediately and drain on paper towels. When cooled, put about 30 meatballs each into five 1-quart freezer containers, leaving ½-inch space at top. Seal and label containers. Freeze. Use within 3 months. Makes about 144 meatballs.

MEATBALL MIX makes:

Cocktail Meatballs, page 111
Spaghetti & Meatballs, page 123
Sweet & Sour Meatballs, page 135
Meatball Stew, page 146

Mexican Meat Mix

Guaranteed to please your guests.

5 lbs. beef roast or combination of beef and pork roasts	2 (7-oz.) cans green chili salsa
3 tablespoons vegetable shortening	¼ teaspoon garlic powder
3 onions, chopped	4 tablespoons flour
1 (4-oz.) can chopped green chilies	4 teaspoons salt
	1 teaspoon ground cumin
	Juices from beef roasts

Preheat oven to 200°F (95°C). Place roasts in large roasting pan or Dutch oven. Do not add salt or water. Cover with a tight lid and roast about 12 hours, until well done. Or cook roasts with 1 cup water in pressure cooker 35 to 40 minutes. Drain meat, reserving juices. Cool meat, then remove bones. Shred meat, and set aside. Melt shortening in a large skillet. Add onions and green chilies. Sauté 1 minute. Add green chili salsa, garlic powder, flour, salt and cumin. Cook 1 minute over medium-low heat. Stir in reserved meat juices and shredded meat. Cook 5 minutes until thick. Cool. Put about 3 cups mix each into three 1-quart containers, leaving ½-inch space at top. Seal and label containers. Freeze. Use within 6 months. Makes about 9 cups of MEXICAN MEAT MIX.

MEXICAN MEAT MIX makes:

Green Chili Burros,
  page 137
Chalupa, page 137
Chimichangas, pages
  138–139

Sour Cream Enchiladas,
  page 141
Tacos Supreme, pages
  141–142

Italian Cooking Sauce Mix

Superb, savory and simple.

2 (14½-oz.) cans stewed
  tomatoes, pureed
4 (8-oz.) cans tomato
  sauce
2 cups water
2 (6-oz.) cans tomato
  paste
2 tablespoons instant
  minced onion
2 tablespoons parsley
  flakes

3 teaspoons salt
2 tablespoons cornstarch
4 teaspoons green pepper
  flakes
1 teaspoon instant
  minced garlic
3 teaspoons sugar
1½ teaspoons Italian
  seasoning

Combine all ingredients in a large kettle or Dutch oven. Simmer 15 minutes over medium-low heat. Cool. Put into six 1-pint freezer containers, leaving ½-inch space at top. Seal and label containers. Freeze. Use within 6 months. Makes about 6 pints of ITALIAN COOKING SAUCE MIX.

ITALIAN COOKING SAUCE MIX makes:

Spaghetti & Meatballs, page 123

Stuffed Manicotti Shells, pages 123–124

Veal Parmigiana, page 124

Chicken Cacciatore, page 129

Last-Minute Lasagne, page 149

Italian Meat Sauce Mix

Well worth the extra effort for authentic Italian dishes.

1 lb. mild Italian sausage, peeled and crumbled
2 lbs. lean ground beef
4 teaspoons salt
¼ teaspoon pepper
½ teaspoon instant minced garlic
1 small onion, peeled
1 carrot, peeled
Water
2 tablespoons sweet basil leaves

¼ teaspoon chili powder
¼ teaspoon thyme
1 (10-oz.) pkg. frozen cauliflower
1 (10-oz.) pkg. frozen broccoli
1 (29-oz.) can tomato puree
1 (12-oz.) can tomato paste
8 cups water

In a large kettle or Dutch oven, brown Italian sausage, ground beef, salt, pepper and minced garlic. Drain. Put onion and carrot in blender. Cover with water, and finely chop. Drain off water and add onion and carrot to meat in kettle. Continue cooking with meat mixture. Stir in basil, chili powder, thyme, cauliflower and broccoli. Add tomato puree, tomato paste and 8 cups water. Bring to a boil. Cover and simmer 8 hours. Skim off fat. Put into eight or nine 1-pint freezer containers, leaving ½-inch space at top. Seal and label containers. Freeze. Use within 6 months. Makes about 8 to 9 pints of ITALIAN MEAT SAUCE MIX.

ITALIAN MEAT SAUCE MIX makes:

Spaghetti & Meatballs, page 123

Stuffed Manicotti Shells, pages 123–124

Last-Minute Lasagne, page 149

Chicken Mix

Deboning chicken isn't much trouble if you do it all at once.

11 lbs. chicken (4 medium fryers), cut up

4 qts. cold water

3 tablespoons parsley flakes

4 carrots, peeled and chopped

4 teaspoons salt

½ teaspoon pepper

2 teaspoons basil

Combine all ingredients in a large kettle or Dutch oven. Cover and cook over high heat until water boils. Simmer until meat is tender, about 1½ hours. Remove from heat. Strain broth and refrigerate until fat can be skimmed. Cool chicken, then remove and discard bones and skin. Put chicken into six 1-pint freezer containers, leaving ½-inch space at top. Pour skimmed chicken broth into six more 1-pint containers, with ½-inch space at top. Seal and label containers. Freeze. Use within 3 months. Makes about 6 pints of CHICKEN MIX and about 6 pints of CHICKEN BROTH.

CHICKEN MIX makes:

Chicken Burgers, 132
Hawaiian Haystack,
    page 132
Sweet & Sour Chicken,
    page 133
Chicken Continental,
    page 155
Club Chicken Casserole,
    pages 155–156

Mexican Chicken Bake,
    page 157
Chicken A La King,
    page 159
Chicken-Cashew
    Casserole, pages
    159–160
Hot Chicken Salad,
    page 160

Herbed Stuffing Mix

*Keep this handy on the shelf
for meat stuffing or tossed salad croutons!*

30 slices firm-textured
    bread, cut in ½-inch
    cubes
⅓ cup cooking oil
3 tablespoons instant
    minced onion

3 tablespoons parsley
    flakes
2 teaspoons garlic salt
¾ teaspoon ground sage
½ teaspoon seasoned
    pepper

Preheat oven to 300°F (150°C). Put bread cubes in
two 13″ × 9″ baking pans. Toast bread cubes in oven
for 45 minutes, stirring occasionally. Remove from
oven and cool slightly. Stir in oil, onion, parsley flakes,
garlic salt, sage and seasoned pepper. Lightly toss
bread cubes with seasonings to coat cubes. Put in a
large airtight container. Label. Store in a cool, dry
place. Use within 3 to 4 months. Makes about 12 cups
of HERBED STUFFING MIX.

HERBED STUFFING MIX makes:

Chicken Oahu, page 131
Supper Stuffing, page 144
Chicken Strata, pages
    156–157

Zucchini Casserole,
    page 162
Scallop Casserole, page
    163

Garden Vegetable Mix

You grew them yourself!

6 cups water
¼ teaspoon garlic
  powder
1 tablespoon salt
1½ teaspoons dried basil
1 medium head cabbage,
  shredded (6 to 8 cups)
1 lb. fresh green beans,
  stemmed, cut in 1-inch
  pieces

3 cups chopped celery
2 cups chopped carrots
1 (10-oz.) pkg. frozen
  corn
1 (10-oz.) pkg. frozen
  peas

Combine all ingredients in a large kettle or Dutch oven. Fill sink with ice water. Cook vegetables to a full boil over medium heat. Remove from heat. Cool quickly by setting kettle in sink of ice water. Put vegetable mix into four 1-quart freezer containers, leaving ½-inch space at top. Seal and label containers. Freeze. Use within 6 months. Makes about 15 cups of GARDEN VEGETABLE MIX.

GARDEN VEGETABLE MIX makes:

Alphabet-Vegetable
  Soup, pages 114, 242
Vegetable-Cheese Soup,
  page 119
Garden Supper, pages
  144, 242
Spring Vegetable Bake,
  page 163

Or combine with ¼ cup water in a small saucepan, cover and bring to a full boil. Reduce heat and simmer 6 to 8 minutes until crisp-tender.

White Sauce Mix

*White Sauce makes meats and
vegetables into meals fit for a king.*

2 cups instant nonfat dry
   milk, or 1½ cups
   regular nonfat dry
   milk

1 cup all-purpose flour
2 teaspoons salt
1 cup butter or margarine

In a large bowl, combine dry milk, flour and salt. Mix
well. With a pastry blender, cut in butter or margarine
until mixture resembles fine crumbs. Put in a large airtight container. Label. Store in refrigerator. Use within
2 months. Makes 1 quart of WHITE SAUCE MIX,
enough for about 8 cups Basic White Sauce, page 113.

WHITE SAUCE MIX makes:

Basic White Sauce,
   page 113
Cream of Chicken Soup,
   page 114
Eastern Corn Chowder,
   pages 115–117
Hearty New England
   Clam Chowder, page
   118

Company Chicken Roll-
   ups, pages 129–130
Potatoes Au Gratin,
   page 164

Basic Cake Mix

Now you can make a better cake in any flavor!

8 cups (2 lbs.) cake flour
6 cups sugar
¼ cup baking powder

1½ teaspoons salt
2½ cups vegetable
   shortening

In a large bowl, sift together cake flour, sugar, baking
powder and salt. Mix well. With a pastry blender, cut
in shortening until evenly distributed. Put in a large airtight container. Label. Store in a cool, dry place. Use
within 10 to 12 weeks. Makes about 16 cups of BASIC
CAKE MIX.

BASIC CAKE MIX makes:

Gingerbread Mix

You'll have gingerbread as quick as a wink.

8 cups all-purpose flour
2 cups sugar
¼ cup baking powder
1 tablespoon salt
1 teaspoon baking soda

1 teaspoon cloves
1 tablespoon ginger
1 tablespoon cinnamon
2 cups vegetable
shortening

In a large bowl, sift together flour, sugar, baking powder, salt, baking soda, cloves, ginger and cinnamon. Mix well. With a pastry blender, cut in shortening until evenly distributed. Mixture will resemble cornmeal in texture. Put in a large airtight container. Label. Store in a cool, dry place. Use within 10 to 12 weeks. Makes about 13 cups of GINGERBREAD MIX.

Variation

Substitute 2 cups of brown sugar for granulated sugar.

GINGERBREAD MIX makes:

Basic Cookie Mix

*With this versatile mix you gain
time, money and variety.*

8 cups all-purpose flour
2½ cups granulated
  sugar
2 cups brown sugar,
  firmly packed

4 teaspoons salt
1½ teaspoons baking
  soda
3 cups vegetable
  shortening

In a large bowl, combine flour, granulated sugar,
brown sugar, salt and baking soda until well-blended.
With a pastry blender, cut in shortening until evenly
distributed. Put in a large airtight container. Label.
Store in a cool, dry place. Use within 10 to 12 weeks.
Makes about 16 cups of BASIC COOKIE MIX.

BASIC COOKIE MIX makes:

Tropic Macaroons,
  page 176
Snickerdoodles, pages
  179–180
Very Vanilla Cookies,
  pages 171, 238
Chocolate Chip Cookies,
  pages 171–172, 238
Sweet & Spicy Cookies,
  pages 172–173

Banana-Coconut De-
  lights, page 176
Date-Filled Drop
  Cookies, page 177
Peanut Butter Cookies,
  page 180
Lemon-Nut Icebox
  Cookies, page 183
Spicebox Cookies, pages
  183–184

Oatmeal Cookie Mix

Add convenience to your old-fashioned favorites.

4 cups all-purpose flour
4 cups whole-wheat flour
4 teaspoons salt
2 teaspoons baking
  powder
2 teaspoons baking soda

6 cups brown sugar,
  firmly packed
3 cups vegetable
  shortening
8 cups quick rolled oats

In a large bowl, combine all-purpose flour, whole-wheat flour, salt, baking powder and baking soda. Blend well. Stir in brown sugar and mix well. With a pastry blender, cut in shortening until evenly distributed. Stir in oats and mix well. Put in a large air-tight container. Label. Store in a cool, dry place. Use within 10 to 12 weeks. Makes about 24 cups of OAT-MEAL COOKIE MIX.

Variation

Use 8 cups all-purpose flour instead of 4 cups all-purpose flour and 4 cups whole-wheat flour.

OATMEAL COOKIE MIX makes:

Gumdrop Jewels, page 174

Peanut Butter & Honey Cookies, page 173

Spice-Raisin Cookies, page 173

Oatmeal Chippers, page 175

Granola Mix

Serve with milk for breakfast or as a great afternoon snack by itself.

10 cups old-fashioned rolled oats
1 cup wheat germ
½ lb. shredded coconut
2 cups raw sunflower seeds
1 cup sesame seeds
3 cups chopped almonds, pecans, walnuts or combination
1½ cups brown sugar, firmly packed

1½ cups water
1½ cups vegetable oil
½ cup honey
½ cup molasses
1½ teaspoons salt
2 teaspoons cinnamon
3 teaspoons vanilla
Raisins or other dried fruits, if desired

Preheat oven to 300°F (150°C). In a large bowl combine oats, wheat germ, coconut, sunflower seeds, sesame seeds and nuts. Blend well. In a large saucepan, combine brown sugar, water, oil, honey, molasses, salt, cinnamon and vanilla. Heat until sugar is dissolved, but do not boil. Pour syrup over dry ingredients and stir until well-coated. Spread into five 13″ × 9″ baking pans, or cookie sheets with sides. Bake 20 to 30 minutes, stirring occasionally. Bake 15 minutes longer for crunchier texture. Cool. Add raisins or other dried fruit, if desired. Put in airtight containers. Label. Store in a cool, dry place. Use within 6 months. Makes about 20 cups of GRANOLA MIX.

GRANOLA MIX makes:

Gruffins, page 88
Breakfast Cookies,
    pages 175, 238

Magic Granola Bars,
    pages 187, 238

How to Make Granola Mix

1/Oats, coconut, wheat germ, sunflower seeds, sesame seeds and chopped nuts are among the healthful ingredients to include in granola.

2/Pour the syrup of honey, molasses and brown sugar over the dry ingredients and stir to coat well.

Brownie Mix

For a quick after-school treat, keep this handy!

6 cups all-purpose flour
4 teaspoons baking
  powder
4 teaspoons salt
8 cups sugar

1 (8-oz.) can
  unsweetened cocoa
2 cups vegetable
  shortening

In a large bowl, sift together flour, baking powder and salt. Add sugar and cocoa. Blend well. With a pastry blender, cut in shortening until evenly distributed. Put in a large airtight container. Label. Store in a cool, dry place. Use within 10 to 12 weeks. Makes about 17 cups of BROWNIE MIX.

BROWNIE MIX makes:

Chewy Chocolate
  Cookies, pages 172,
  236
Our Best Brownies,
  pages 184–185, 236
Texas Sheet Cake,
  page 208

Fudge Sauce for Cream
  Puffs Supreme, page
  216
Brownie Alaska, page
  222
Mississippi Mud, pages
  223–224

Lemon Pie-Filling Mix

Tart and refreshing for a sauce or filling.

2½ cups presweetened
  powdered lemonade
  mix
1 cup plus 2 tablespoons
  cornstarch

1¼ cups sugar, more for
  sweeter flavor
1 teaspoon salt

In a medium bowl, combine lemonade mix, cornstarch, sugar and salt. Mix well. Put in a 1-quart airtight container. Label. Store in a cool, dry place. Use within 6 to 8 months. Makes about 4¼ cups of LEMON PIE-FILLING MIX.

LEMON PIE-FILLING MIX makes:

Hot Lemon Sauce for Sugar & Spice Gingerbread, pages 200–201, 244

Luscious Lemon Pie, page 211

Pudding & Pie Mix

This will be one of your favorites!

5½ cups sugar
2¾ cups all-purpose flour

1 teaspoon salt
1½ cups instant nonfat dry milk

In a large bowl, combine sugar, flour, salt and dry milk. Mix well. Put in a large airtight container. Label. Store in a cool, dry place. Use within 6 to 8 months. Makes about 9 cups of PUDDING & PIE MIX.

Variation

If you prefer cornstarch puddings, substitute 2 cups cornstarch for all-purpose flour.

PUDDING & PIE MIX makes:

Vanilla Cream Pie, page 212

Chocolate Cream Pie, page 213

Cookie Crumb Crust Mix

In great taste whenever your recipes call for a crumb crust.

6 cups all-purpose flour
1½ cups chopped nuts
1½ cups brown sugar, firmly packed

1 lb. butter or margarine, softened

Preheat oven to 375°F (190°C). In a large bowl, combine flour, nuts and brown sugar. Blend well. With a pastry blender, cut in butter or margarine until mixture resembles cornmeal in texture. Press mixture firmly into 2 unbuttered, shallow baking pans. Bake about 15 minutes. Cool. Crumble and put in a large airtight container. Label. Store in a cool, dry place. Use within 4 to 6 weeks. Makes about 10½ cups of COOKIE CRUMB CRUST MIX.

COOKIE CRUMB CRUST MIX makes:

Cookie Crumb Crust

2 cups COOKIE CRUMB CRUST MIX, see above

Press about 2 cups crumb mix into a baking pan or 9-inch pie plate and bake according to directions for filling.

Flaky Pie Crust Mix

Your guests will remember how light your pies are!

12½ cups all-purpose flour
2 tablespoons salt

5 cups vegetable shortening

Combine flour and salt in a large bowl. Mix well. With a pastry blender, cut in shortening until evenly distributed. Mixture will resemble cornmeal in texture. Put in a large airtight container. Label. Store in a cool, dry place. Use within 10 to 12 weeks. Or put about 2½ cups mixture each into 6 freezer bags. Seal and label bags. Freeze. Use within 12 months. Makes about 16 cups of FLAKY PIE CRUST MIX, enough for 6 double-crust pies or 12 single-crust pies.

Flaky Pie Crust

2½ cups FLAKY PIE
   CRUST MIX, see
   above
¼ cup ice water

1 egg, beaten
1 tablespoon white
   vinegar

Crumble FLAKY PIE CRUST MIX, if frozen. Put mix in a medium bowl. In a small bowl, combine ice water, egg and vinegar. Sprinkle one spoonful of water mixture at a time over the FLAKY PIE CRUST MIX and toss with a fork until the dough barely clings together in the bowl. Roll out dough to desired thickness between 2 sheets of lightly floured wax paper. Place dough in a 9-inch pie plate without stretching. Flute edges. If filling recipe calls for a baked pie crust, preheat oven to 425°F (220°C). Bake 10 to 15 minutes, until very lightly browned. Cool. Fill and bake according to directions for filling. For double-crust pie, place top crust over filling, press and flute edges, and cut slits in top crust. Makes enough crust for one 9-inch double-crust pie or two 9-inch single-crust pies.

FLAKY PIE CRUST makes:

Simplified Quiche,
   page 136
All-American Apple Pie,
   page 210
Luscious Lemon Pie,
   page 211

Vanilla Cream Pie,
   page 212
Chocolate Cream Pie,
   page 213

If you do not have a Dutch oven, try preparing BRAISED BEEF CUBE MIX, MEXICAN MEAT MIX and ITALIAN MEAT SAUCE MIX in a slow cooker. Check the manufacturer's instructions to adjust cooking times.

Moist Pie Crust Mix

Our favorite pie crust—
marvelous to have on hand in your freezer.

20 cups (5 lbs.) all-
   purpose flour
2 tablespoons salt
1 (3-lb.) can vegetable
   shortening

3 cups cold water
¼ cup all-purpose flour,
   if desired

Combine flour and salt in a very large bowl. Mix well.
With pastry blender, cut in shortening until evenly distributed. Mixture will resemble cornmeal in texture.
Add cold water all at once and mix lightly until the
flour absorbs all the water and texture resembles putty.
If dough is too sticky, sprinkle a little flour over the
top and mix until the dough barely clings together in
the bowl. Divide dough into 10 oblong rolls. Wrap
each roll well with plastic wrap and heavy foil. Freeze.
Use within 12 months. Makes 10 rolls of MOIST PIE
CRUST MIX, enough for 10 double-crust pies or 20
single-crust pies.

MOIST PIE CRUST MIX makes:
Sausage Rolls, page 110

Moist Pie Crust

1 roll MOIST PIE
   CRUST MIX,
   see above, partially
   thawed

Divide dough into 2 balls. Roll out dough to desired
thickness between 2 sheets of lightly floured wax paper.
Place dough in a 9-inch pie plate without stretching.
Flute edges. If filling recipe calls for a baked pie crust,
preheat oven to 425°F (220°C). Bake 10 to 15 minutes, until very lightly browned. Cool. Fill and bake

according to directions for filling. For double-crust pie, place top crust over filling, press and flute edges, and cut slits in top crust. Makes enough for one 9-inch double-crust pie or two 9-inch single-crust pies.

MOIST PIE CRUST makes:

How to Make Moist Pie Crust

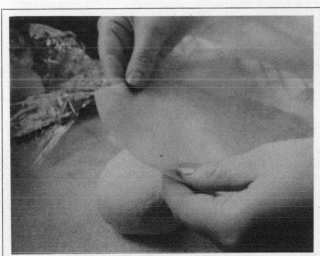

1/Thaw a roll of MOIST PIE CRUST MIX and divide it into 2 balls. This is enough for 1 double-crust pie or 2 single-crust pies.

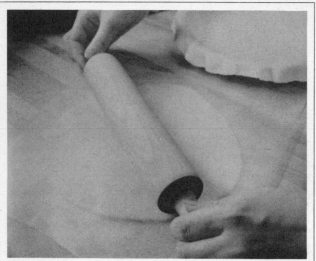

2/Roll the dough to the desired thickness and size between 2 sheets of lightly floured wax paper.

3/Do not stretch the pie crust dough as you place it in the pie plate. Pour in the filling, place the top crust over the filling and flute the edges.

SPECIAL MIXES

Special Mixes differ from Master Mixes in that they are designed primarily for one recipe while Master Mixes make several recipes. This is where you'll find the seasoning mixes, salad dressing mixes, beverages, dips and side dishes. The recipe made by each Special Mix follows the mix itself. Most of the Special Mixes are dry mixes which keep about 6 months.

You will note that Special Mixes resemble commercial seasoning mixes you find on your grocer's shelves. They can be used whenever you would use a similar packaged mix. The advantages of making your own Special Mixes rather than purchasing them are fresher flavor, lower cost and lack of additives.

With the exception of the beverage mixes, most Special Mixes should be stored in proportions for individual recipes for your convenience. Foil packets are great for this purpose. The dry beverage mixes are most easily stored in large canisters. Remember that HOT CHOCOLATE MIX makes 34 cups of mix, enough for 100 cups of Hot Chocolate! FRUIT SLUSH MIX and MARIE'S FRUIT COCKTAIL MIX should be frozen according to recipe directions.

For added convenience, try storing the Salad Dressing Mixes in containers large enough for you to add the remaining ingredients. Then you can just shake them up at serving time! It makes Make-A-Mix Cookery even easier.

When preparing Special Mixes, remember to label them before storing. They are often difficult to distinguish from one another later.

We know you will enjoy having Special Mixes made ahead and ready on your shelves. Start making extra batches of your favorites. Our favorites include HOME-STYLE DRESSING MIX, MARIE'S FRUIT COCKTAIL MIX and CHICKEN-FLAVORED RICE MIX. Try all the rice mixes for some flavor surprises. When you serve the dip mixes at a party, be sure to have copies of the recipe close at hand. These dips guarantee "rave reviews."

Let's Make Gifts, page 230, has ideas on how to use both Master Mixes and Special Mixes as gifts for any occasion.

Russian Refresher Mix

An imitation Russian tea—without the tea!

2 cups powdered orange
   drink mix
1 (3-oz.) pkg. pre-
   sweetened powdered
   lemonade mix

1⅓ cups sugar
1 teaspoon cinnamon
½ teaspoon ground
   cloves

Combine all ingredients in a medium bowl. Mix well. Put in a 1-quart airtight container. Label. Store in a cool, dry place. Use within 6 months. Makes about 3½ cups of RUSSIAN REFRESHER MIX.

Russian Refresher

Add 2 to 3 teaspoons of RUSSIAN REFRESHER MIX, see above, to 1 cup hot water. Stir to dissolve. Makes 1 serving.

Hot Chocolate Mix

The camper's favorite.

1 (25.6-oz.) pkg. instant
   nonfat dry milk (10⅔
   cups)
1 (6-oz.) jar powdered
   non-dairy creamer

2 cups powdered sugar
1 (16-oz.) can instant
   chocolate drink mix

Combine all ingredients in a large bowl. Mix well. Put in a large airtight container. Label. Store in a cool, dry place. Use within 6 months. Makes about 17 cups of HOT CHOCOLATE MIX.

Hot Chocolate

Add 3 tablespoons HOT CHOCOLATE MIX, see above, to 1 cup hot water. Stir to dissolve. Makes 1 serving.

Orange Float Mix

A frothy, refreshing delight!

4 cups instant nonfat   1 cup sugar
  dry milk
2 cups powdered orange
  drink mix

Combine ingredients in a large bowl. Blend well. Put in a large airtight container. Label. Store in a cool, dry place. Use within 6 months. Makes about 7 cups of ORANGE FLOAT MIX.

Orange Float

Add 1 egg and ½ cup of ORANGE FLOAT MIX, see above, to 8 ounces of cold water in blender. Add 2 to 3 ice cubes and blend well. Serve immediately. Makes 1 serving.

Fruit Slush Mix

A quick, cool, refreshing drink—
right from your freezer.

4 cups sugar   ½ cup lemon juice
4 cups water   1 (46-oz.) can pine-
1 (6-oz.) can frozen   apple juice
  orange juice
  concentrate

For frosty cold drink glasses, store the glasses in the freezer about 30 minutes before serving.

Combine sugar and water in a medium saucepan. Heat until sugar is dissolved. Add orange juice concentrate, lemon juice and pineapple juice. Fill 6 or 7 ice cube trays with mixture. Freeze until firm. Remove cubes from freezer trays and store in plastic bags. Use within 6 months. Makes about 100 small cubes.

Variation

Add 5 to 6 mashed bananas to mixture before freezing.

Fruit Slush

Fill a glass with FRUIT SLUSH MIX cubes, see above. Add ginger ale to cover. Let stand 15 minutes. Stir and serve. Makes 1 serving.

Marie's Fruit Cocktail Mix

When summer fruits are at their peak, prepare this mix for future use.

4 cups sugar	2 crenshaw melons, cut in chunks
2 qts. water	
1 (6-oz.) can frozen orange juice concentrate	3 lbs. green grapes
	3 lbs. peaches, cut in chunks
1 (6-oz.) can frozen lemonade concentrate	1 lb. blueberries, fresh or frozen
1 watermelon, cut in balls	
2 cantaloupes, cut in chunks	

In a large saucepan bring sugar and water to a boil, stirring constantly. Stir in frozen orange juice concentrate and frozen lemonade concentrate. In a large bowl combine watermelon, cantaloupes, crenshaw melons, grapes, peaches and blueberries. Put mixed fruit in twelve 1-pint freezer containers, leaving ½-inch space at top. Pour hot juice syrup over top. Seal and label containers. Freeze. Use within 6 to 8 months. Makes about 12 pints of MARIE'S FRUIT COCKTAIL MIX.

Marie's Fruit Cocktail

Partially thaw 1 pint of MARIE'S FRUIT COCKTAIL MIX, see above. Spoon into fruit cups. Pour ginger ale over top, if desired. Makes 4 servings.

Chicken-Flavored Rice Mix

An excellent addition to your favorite main dish.

4 cups uncooked long-grain rice	2 teaspoons dried tarragon
4 tablespoons instant chicken bouillon	2 teaspoons dried parsley flakes
1 teaspoon salt	¼ teaspoon white pepper

Combine all ingredients in a large bowl. Stir until evenly distributed. Put about 1⅓ cups mixture each into three 1-pint airtight containers. Label. Store in a cool, dry place. Use within 6 to 8 months. Makes about 4 cups of CHICKEN-FLAVORED RICE MIX.

Chicken-Flavored Rice

1⅓ cups CHICKEN-FLAVORED RICE MIX, see above	2 cups cold water
	1 tablespoon butter or margarine

Combine all ingredients in a medium saucepan. Bring to a boil over high heat. Cover, reduce heat and cook 15 minutes, until liquid is absorbed. Makes 4 to 6 servings.

Dill-Lemon Rice Mix

Serve this as a side dish with fresh trout!

4 cups uncooked long-
    grain rice
5 teaspoons dried grated
    lemon peel
4 teaspoons dill weed or
    dill seed

2 teaspoons dried
    minced chives
2 teaspoons salt
8 teaspoons instant
    chicken bouillon

Combine all ingredients in a large bowl. Stir until evenly distributed. Put about 1½ cups mixture each into three 1-pint airtight containers. Label. Store in a cool, dry place. Use within 6 to 8 months. Makes about 4½ cups of DILL-LEMON RICE MIX.

Dill-Lemon Rice

1½ cups DILL-LEMON
    RICE MIX, see above
2 cups cold water

1 tablespoon butter or
    margarine

Combine ingredients in a medium saucepan. Bring to a boil over high heat. Cover, reduce heat and cook 15 minutes, until liquid is absorbed. Makes 4 to 6 servings.

Onion-Flavored Rice Mix

Special flavor for a side dish or casserole.

4 cups uncooked long-
    grain rice
2 (1¼-oz.) pkgs. onion
    soup mix

1 tablespoon parsley
    flakes
1 teaspoon salt

Combine ingredients in a large bowl. Stir until evenly distributed. Put about 1⅓ cups mixture each into three 1-pint airtight containers. Label. Store in a cool, dry place. Use within 6 to 8 months. Makes about 4 cups of ONION-FLAVORED RICE MIX.

Onion-Flavored Rice

1⅓ cups ONION-
   FLAVORED RICE
   MIX, see above

2 cups cold water
1 tablespoon butter or
   margarine

Combine ingredients in a medium saucepan. Bring to a boil over high heat. Cover, reduce heat and cook 15 minutes, until liquid is absorbed. Makes 4 to 6 servings.

Mexican Rice Mix

You may find yourself making this every week!

4 cups uncooked long-
   grain rice
½ cup green pepper
   flakes

4 teaspoons salt
5 teaspoons parsley flakes
1 teaspoon dried basil

Combine all ingredients in a large bowl. Stir until evenly distributed. Put about 1½ cups mixture each into three 1-pint airtight containers. Label. Store in a cool, dry place. Use within 6 to 8 months. Makes about 4½ cups of MEXICAN RICE MIX.

Mexican Rice

1½ cups MEXICAN
   RICE MIX, see above
2 cups cold water

1 tablespoon butter or
   margarine

Combine ingredients in a medium saucepan. Bring to a boil over high heat. Cover, reduce heat and cook 15 minutes, until liquid is absorbed. Makes 4 to 6 servings.

Vegetarian Rice Mix

The blend of flavors is intriguing.

4 cups uncooked long-grain rice
3 tablespoons instant vegetarian bouillon
2 teaspoons salt
4 teaspoons celery flakes
4 teaspoons onion flakes
4 teaspoons green pepper flakes
4 teaspoons red pepper flakes

Combine all ingredients in a large bowl. Stir until evenly distributed. Put about 1½ cups mixture each into three 1-pint airtight containers. Label. Store in a cool, dry place. Use within 6 to 8 months. Makes about 4½ cups of VEGETARIAN RICE MIX.

Vegetarian Rice

1½ cups VEGETARIAN RICE MIX, see above
2 cups cold water
1 tablespoon butter or margarine

Combine ingredients in a medium saucepan. Bring to a boil over high heat. Cover, reduce heat and cook 15 minutes, until liquid is absorbed. Makes 4 to 6 servings.

Caesar Salad Dressing Mix

A traditional favorite. Don't forget the HERBED STUFFING MIX croutons, page 28.

1½ teaspoons grated lemon peel
1 teaspoon oregano
⅛ teaspoon instant minced garlic
2 tablespoons grated Parmesan cheese
½ teaspoon pepper

Combine all ingredients in a small bowl until evenly distributed. Put mixture in a foil packet or 1-pint glass jar. Label. Store in a cool, dry place. Use within 3 to 4 months. Makes about 3 tablespoons CAESAR SALAD DRESSING MIX, enough for ¾ cup Caesar Salad Dressing.

Caesar Salad Dressing

1 recipe CAESAR SALAD DRESSING MIX, see above	½ cup vegetable oil ¼ cup lemon juice

Combine ingredients in a glass jar. Shake until well-blended. Chill before serving. Makes about ¾ cup of Caesar Salad Dressing.

French Dressing Mix

The all-time favorite.

¼ cup sugar	1½ teaspoons salt
1½ teaspoons paprika	⅛ teaspoon onion
1 teaspoon dry mustard	powder

Combine all ingredients in a small bowl until evenly distributed. Put mixture in a foil packet or 1-pint glass jar. Label. Store in a cool, dry place. Use within 6 months. Makes about 5 tablespoons FRENCH DRESSING MIX, enough for 1¼ cups French Dressing.

Variation

Sweet Italian Dressing: Increase sugar to ½ cup. Substitute 1 tablespoon celery seed for paprika.

French Dressing

1 recipe FRENCH DRESSING MIX, see above	¾ cup vegetable oil ¼ cup vinegar

Combine ingredients in a glass jar. Shake until well-blended. Chill before serving. Makes about ¼ cups of French Dressing.

Super Salad Seasoning Mix

You'll find more and more ways to use it!

2 cups grated Parmesan cheese
2 teaspoons salt
½ cup sesame seed
½ teaspoon garlic salt
1 tablespoon instant minced onion
2 tablespoons parsley flakes
½ teaspoon dried dill seed
2 tablespoons poppy seeds
1 teaspoon monosodium glutamate, if desired
3 tablespoons celery seed
2 teaspoons paprika
½ teaspoon fresh ground pepper

Combine all ingredients in a small bowl. Mix until evenly distributed. Put in a 1-quart airtight container. Label. Store in a cool, dry place. Use within 3 to 4 months. Makes about 3 cups SUPER SALAD SEASONING MIX.

SUPER SALAD SEASONING MIX makes:

Sprinkled topping over tossed green salads, baked potatoes, and buttered French bread or rolls, before toasting.

Garnish for potato salads, macaroni or egg salads.
Sour cream dip made with 2 tablespoons mix and 1 cup sour cream.

How to Make & Use
Super Salad Seasoning Mix

1/For an all-purpose seasoning, combine
Parmesan cheese, sesame seeds, parsley flakes,
dried dill seed, celery seed and other spices.

2/Keep some SUPER SALAD SEASONING MIX
in a shaker to sprinkle over baked potatoes, salads
or toasted and buttered French bread or rolls.

3/Combine 2 tablespoons seasoning mix
with 1 cup sour cream to make a tasty dip
for chips and vegetables.

Sweet Salad Dressing Mix

Toss it with crisp greens or serve with fresh fruit.

⅓ cup sugar
1 teaspoon instant
  minced onion
1 teaspoon salt

1 teaspoon dry mustard
1 teaspoon paprika
1 teaspoon celery seed

Combine all ingredients in a small bowl until evenly distributed. Put mixture in a foil packet or 1-pint glass jar. Label. Store in a cool, dry place. Use within 6 months. Makes about ½ cup of SWEET SALAD DRESSING MIX, enough for 1¼ cups Sweet Salad Dressing.

Sweet Salad Dressing

1 recipe SWEET SALAD
  DRESSING MIX,
  see above

¾ cup vegetable oil
¼ cup vinegar

Combine ingredients in a glass jar. Stir until well-blended. Chill before serving. Makes about 1¼ cups Sweet Salad Dressing.

Home-Style Dressing Mix

Your own version of that famous dressing.

2 teaspoons instant
  minced onion
½ teaspoon salt
⅛ teaspoon garlic
  powder

½ teaspoon mono-
  sodium glutamate, if
  desired
1 tablespoon parsley
  flakes

Combine all ingredients in a small bowl until evenly distributed. Put mixture in a foil packet or 1-pint glass jar. Label. Store in a cool, dry place. Use within 6 months. Makes about 2 tablespoons of HOME-STYLE DRESSING MIX, enough for 2 cups Home-Style Dressing.

Home-Style Dressing

1 recipe HOME-STYLE
DRESSING MIX,
see above

1 cup mayonnaise
1 cup buttermilk

Combine ingredients in a glass jar. Shake until well-blended. Chill before serving. Makes about 2 cups Home-Style Dressing.

Variation

Substitute 1 cup sour cream for buttermilk and use as a dip for fresh vegetables.

Low-Calorie Dressing Mix

For weight-watchers, this fills the bill.

2 teaspoons instant
minced onion
2 teaspoons parsley flakes
¼ teaspoon instant
horseradish

2 teaspoons green pepper
flakes

Combine all ingredients in a small bowl until evenly distributed. Put mixture in a foil packet or 1-pint glass jar. Label. Store in a cool, dry place. Use within 6 months. Makes about 2 tablespoons LOW-CALORIE DRESSING MIX, enough for ¾ cup Low-Calorie Dressing.

Low-Calorie Dressing

1 recipe LOW-
CALORIE DRESS-
ING MIX, see above

¾ cup tomato juice
2 tablespoons lemon
juice

Combine ingredients in a glass jar. Shake until well-blended. Chill before serving. Makes about ¾ cup Low-Calorie Dressing.

Chicken Coating Mix

Better than your favorite restaurant makes!

2 tablespoons parsley
  flakes
1 tablespoon oregano
1 tablespoon marjoram
1 tablespoon thyme
2 teaspoons rosemary
1 teaspoon garlic salt

1 teaspoon onion salt
1 tablespoon celery salt
1 tablespoon ginger
1 teaspoon pepper
1 teaspoon sage
1 tablespoon paprika

Combine all ingredients in a small bowl until evenly distributed. Spoon mixture into a small airtight container. Label. Store in a cool, dry place. Use within 6 months. Makes about ½ cup of CHICKEN COATING MIX.

Oven-Fried Chicken

1½ teaspoons
  CHICKEN COATING
  MIX, see above
¾ cup all-purpose flour
¼ cup instant nonfat
  dry milk
2 teaspoons sugar
1 teaspoon baking
  powder

½ teaspoon salt
⅔ cup hot water
2 tablespoons vegetable
  oil
1 (2½- to 3-lb.) fryer
  chicken, cut up

Preheat oven to 425°F (220°C). Combine all ingredients except chicken in a small bowl. Blend well. Dip chicken pieces in batter and place on a baking sheet. Bake uncovered 40 to 50 minutes, until golden brown and tender. Or if desired, dip chicken pieces in batter then fry in hot oil.

Variation

Coat chicken with CHICKEN COATING MIX and 1 cup flour, then fry in hot oil.

Substitute 1 cup PANCAKE MIX, page 19, or packaged pancake mix for flour, dry milk, sugar, baking powder and salt.

Seafood Coating Mix

A great flavor combination for fish.

2 tablespoons parsley flakes	1 tablespoon thyme
	1 tablespoon marjoram
1 tablespoon dried grated lemon peel	1 teaspoon onion salt
	1 bay leaf, crushed
1 tablespoon celery seed	1 teaspoon monosodium
1 tablespoon savory salt	glutamate, if desired

Combine all ingredients in a small bowl evenly distributed. Put mixture in a small airtight container. Label. Store in a cool, dry place. Use within 6 months. Makes about ⅓ cup of SEAFOOD COATING MIX.

Breaded Seafood

1 tablespoon SEAFOOD COATING MIX, see above	Fish fillets or seafood Butter or vegetable oil for frying
½ cup flour or dry breadcrumbs	

Combine SEAFOOD COATING MIX and flour or breadcrumbs in a pie plate or shallow dish. Coat fish fillets or any seafood mixture. Pan fry in butter until golden brown. Or preheat oil in a deep-fryer to 375°F (190°C) and fry 3 to 5 minutes until golden brown.

Seasoned Breadcrumb Mix

How many uses can you think of?

2 cups fine dry bread-
  crumbs (4 slices bread)
⅓ cup instant minced
  onion
1 tablespoon parsley
  flakes
1 tablespoon seasoned
  salt

1 teaspoon salt
½ teaspoon pepper
1½ teaspoons mono-
  sodium glutamate, if
  desired
1 teaspoon Italian
  seasoning

Combine all ingredients in a medium bowl until evenly
distributed. Put in a 1-quart airtight container. Label.
Store in a cool, dry place. Use within 6 months. Makes
about 2½ cups of SEASONED BREADCRUMB
MIX.

SEASONED BREADCRUMB MIX makes:

Breading for pork chops,
  chicken, fish, cube
  steaks and fresh vege-
  tables, before frying.

Filler for meat loaf or
  salmon loaf.

Chili Seasoning Mix

You'd better double the recipe!

1 tablespoon all-purpose
  flour
2 tablespoons instant
  minced onion
1½ teaspoons chili
  - powder
1 teaspoon seasoned salt

½ teaspoon crushed
  dried red pepper
½ teaspoon instant
  minced garlic
½ teaspoon sugar
½ teaspoon ground
  cumin

Combine all ingredients in a small bowl until evenly
distributed. Spoon mixture onto a 6-inch square of
aluminum foil and fold to make airtight. Label. Store

in a cool, dry place. Use within 6 months. Makes 1 package (about ¼ cup) of CHILI SEASONING MIX. To make additional packages, increase ingredient amounts proportionately.

Variation

For a special treat, sprinkle CHILI SEASONING MIX over hot popcorn.

Chili

1 lb. lean ground beef
2 (15½-oz.) cans kidney beans

2 (16-oz.) cans tomatoes
1 pkg. CHILI SEASON-ING MIX, see above

Brown ground beef in a medium skillet over medium-high heat. Drain. Add kidney beans, tomatoes and CHILI SEASONING MIX. Reduce heat and simmer 10 minutes, stirring occasionally. Makes 4 to 6 servings.

Store each salad dressing mix in a 1-pint glass jar with a screw-top lid. When you're ready to make salad dressing, just add the liquid ingredients, shake and chill.

Spaghetti Seasoning Mix

It makes great lasagne and pizza sauce, too!

1 tablespoon instant minced onion
1 tablespoon parsley flakes
1 tablespoon cornstarch
2 teaspoons green pepper flakes
1½ teaspoons salt
¼ teaspoon instant minced garlic
1 teaspoon sugar
¾ teaspoon Italian seasoning or combination of Italian herbs (oregano, basil, rosemary, thyme, sage, marjoram)

Combine all ingredients in a small bowl until evenly distributed. Spoon mixture onto a 6-inch square of aluminum foil and fold to make airtight. Label. Store in a cool, dry place. Use within 6 months. Makes 1 package (about ⅓ cup) SPAGHETTI SEASONING MIX.

Spaghetti Sauce

1 lb. lean ground beef
2 (8-oz.) cans tomato sauce
1 (6-oz.) can tomato paste
2¾ cups tomato juice or water
1 pkg. SPAGHETTI SEASONING MIX, see above

Brown ground beef in a medium skillet over medium-high heat. Drain excess grease. Add tomato sauce, tomato paste and tomato juice or water. Stir in SPAGHETTI SEASONING MIX. Reduce heat and simmer 30 minutes, stirring occasionally. Makes 4 to 6 servings.

Sloppy Joe Seasoning Mix

So easy and so good!

1 tablespoon instant
  minced onion
1 teaspoon green pepper
  flakes
1 teaspoon salt
1 teaspoon cornstarch

½ teaspoon instant
  minced garlic
¼ teaspoon dry mustard
¼ teaspoon celery seed
¼ teaspoon chili powder

Combine all ingredients in a small bowl until evenly distributed. Spoon mixture onto a 6-inch square of aluminum foil and fold to make airtight. Label. Store in a cool, dry place. Use within 6 months. Makes 1 package (about 3 tablespoons) SLOPPY JOE SEASONING MIX.

Sloppy Joes

1 lb. lean ground beef
1 pkg. SLOPPY JOE
  SEASONING MIX,
  see above
½ cup water

1 (8-oz.) can tomato
  sauce
6 hamburger buns,
  toasted

Brown ground beef in a medium skillet over medium-high heat. Drain excess grease. Add SLOPPY JOE SEASONING MIX, water and tomato sauce. Bring to a boil. Reduce heat and simmer 10 minutes, stirring occasionally. Serve over toasted hamburger buns. Makes 6 servings.

Taco Seasoning Mix

Your tacos will be hot and spicy!

2 teaspoons instant
  minced onion
1 teaspoon salt
1 teaspoon chili powder
½ teaspoon cornstarch
½ teaspoon crushed
  dried red pepper

½ teaspoon instant
  minced garlic
¼ teaspoon dried
  oregano
½ teaspoon ground
  cumin

Combine all ingredients in a small bowl until evenly distributed. Spoon mixture onto a 6-inch square of aluminum foil and fold to make airtight. Label. Store in a cool, dry place. Use within 6 months. Makes 1 package (about 2 tablespoons) TACO SEASONING MIX. To make additional packages, increase ingredient amounts proportionately.

Taco Filling

1 lb. lean ground beef
½ cup water

1 pkg. TACO SEASON-
  ING MIX, see above

Brown ground beef in a medium skillet over medium-high heat. Drain excess grease. Add water and TACO SEASONING MIX. Reduce heat and simmer 10 minutes, stirring occasionally. Makes filling for 8 to 10 tacos.

Bacon-Flavored Dip Mix

Your guests will choose this dip first.

2 tablespoons instant
  bacon bits
1 tablespoon instant
  minced onion

1 teaspoon instant beef
  bouillon
⅛ teaspoon minced
  garlic

Combine all ingredients in a small bowl until evenly distributed. Spoon mixture onto a 6-inch square of aluminum foil and fold to make airtight. Label. Store in a cool, dry place. Use within 6 months. Makes 1 package (about 3 tablespoons) of BACON-FLAVORED DIP MIX. To make additional packages, increase ingredient amounts proportionately.

Bacon-Flavored Dip

1 cup sour cream
1 pkg. BACON-
    FLAVORED DIP
    MIX, see above

Combine sour cream and BACON-FLAVORED DIP MIX. Chill at least 1 hour before serving. Makes about 1 cup Bacon-Flavored Dip.

Variations

Substitute 1 cup yogurt, 1 cup cottage cheese, or 1 (8-oz.) package softened cream cheese for sour cream.

Sesame-Cheese Dip Mix

The flavor of sesame seeds makes this a favorite.

1 tablespoon grated
    Parmesan cheese
2 teaspoons toasted
    sesame seeds
½ teaspoon salt

½ teaspoon celery seed
Dash pepper
⅛ teaspoon garlic
    powder

Combine all ingredients in a small bowl until evenly distributed. Spoon mixture onto a 6-inch square of aluminum foil and fold to make airtight. Label. Store in a cool, dry place. Use within 3 to 4 months. Makes 1 package (about 2 tablespoons) SESAME-CHEESE DIP MIX. To make additional packages, increase ingredient amounts proportionately.

Sesame-Cheese Dip

1 cup sour cream
2 tablespoons SESAME-
   CHEESE DIP MIX,
   see above

Combine sour cream and SESAME-CHEESE DIP MIX. Chill at least 1 hour before serving. Makes about 1 cup Sesame-Cheese Dip.

Variation
Substitute 1 cup yogurt for sour cream.

Onion-Cheese Dip Mix

Let your vegetables take a dip in this!

1 tablespoon instant
   minced onion
1 tablespoon grated
   Parmesan cheese

1½ teaspoons instant
   beef bouillon
¼ teaspoon garlic salt

Combine all ingredients in a small bowl until evenly distributed. Spoon mixture onto a 6-inch square of aluminum foil and fold to make airtight. Label. Store in a cool, dry place. Use within 3 to 4 months. Makes 1 package (about 3 tablespoons) ONION-CHEESE DIP MIX. To make additional packages, increase ingredient amounts proportionately.

Onion-Cheese Dip

1 cup sour cream
1 pkg. ONION-CHEESE
   DIP MIX, see above

Combine sour cream and ONION-CHEESE DIP MIX.
Chill at least 1 hour before serving. Makes about 1 cup
of Onion-Cheese Dip.

Variations

Substitute 1 cup cottage cheese or 1 (8-oz.) package
softened cream cheese for sour cream.

Vegetable Dip Mix

The ideal place to put fresh garden vegetables.

1 tablespoon dried   1 teaspoon garlic salt
   chives   ½ teaspoon paprika
½ teaspoon dill weed

Combine all ingredients in a small bowl until evenly
distributed. Spoon mixture onto a 6-inch square of
aluminum foil and fold to make airtight. Label. Store
in a cool, dry place. Use within 6 months. Makes 1
package (about 2 tablespoons) of VEGETABLE DIP
MIX. To make additional packages, increase ingredient
amounts proportionately.

Vegetable Dip

1 tablespoon lemon juice   1 pkg. VEGETABLE
1 cup mayonnaise   DIP MIX, see
1 cup sour cream   above

Combine all ingredients. Chill at least 1 hour before
serving. Makes about 2 cups of Vegetable Dip.

BREAKFAST & BRUNCH

The aroma of freshly baked muffins coming from your kitchen is the best way to wake up your family in a very pleasant way. Is it too hard for you to get things baking soon enough to do that? With Master Mixes on your pantry shelf, you have a whole collection of Breakfast & Brunch delights to serve to your family or guests in minutes. You already know that a well-balanced breakfast contributes to your family's well-being throughout the day. A mix you've made is a great way to begin those easy, nutritious meals.

The Swedish Cinnamon Twists in the cover photo are beautiful rolls that look fancy but are easy to make with HOT ROLL MIX. Serve this treat with a favorite beverage and fruit.

Look closely at the rolls and breads in this chapter and Breads & Rolls, page 93. By making the basic dough from HOT ROLL MIX, you can finish a variety of baked goods, such as Cinnamon Rolls, Cream Cheese Swirls and Orange Butterflake Rolls.

Favorite Wheat Pancakes is our number one choice for breakfast. Serve these light, tender pancakes with a variety of toppings. You won't believe how wonderful they taste. Puff Oven Pancakes create a brunch spectacular right before your eyes. Try them for a late evening supper, too. For best results, we suggest you let pancake batters stand about 5 minutes before cooking.

Serve Gruffins—that's granola muffins—with a cold

glass of milk for a complete breakfast you can eat in a hurry. You'll feel healthy, too. How about some muffins with apples or oatmeal or molasses in them? For those special occasions when your "sweet tooth" yearns for bake shop treats, make some Sunshine Coffee Cake, Butterscotch Butter Balls or Mary's Honey-Walnut Swirl. They'll sure have fun pulling apart the Pluckit!

Swedish Cinnamon Twists

A mouth-watering experience!

1 pkg. active dry yeast
1 tablespoon sugar
¼ cup warm water
1 cup buttermilk
¼ teaspoon baking soda
½ cup butter or
  margarine, melted
2 eggs, beaten

4 to 5 cups HOT ROLL
  MIX, page 17
Cinnamon Filling, see
  below
3 tablespoons butter or
  margarine, melted
Powdered Sugar Glaze,
  see below

Cinnamon Filling:

½ cup brown sugar,
  firmly packed

½ teaspoon cinnamon
½ cup chopped nuts

Powdered Sugar Glaze:

1½ cups sifted powdered
  sugar
½ tablespoon butter or
  margarine, melted

2 tablespoons hot water

In a small bowl, dissolve yeast and sugar in warm water. Set aside. Bring buttermilk to a boil in a small saucepan; buttermilk should curdle. In a large bowl, combine buttermilk, baking soda and ½ cup melted butter or margarine. Add eggs. When mixture is luke-warm, add dissolved yeast mixture. Gradually stir in 4 cups HOT ROLL MIX until the soft dough forms a ball. On a lightly floured surface, knead dough about 5 minutes until smooth and elastic. Add additional HOT ROLL MIX if necessary to make a soft, but not too sticky dough. Lightly butter bowl. Put dough in bowl and turn to butter top. Cover dough with a damp towel and let rise in a warm place until doubled in bulk, about 1 hour. Generously grease 2 baking sheets. Prepare Cinnamon Filling. Punch down dough. Roll out to a 12″ × 20″ rectangle. Brush dough with 3 table-spoons melted butter or margarine. Sprinkle Cinnamon Filling lengthwise over half of dough to within ½ inch of long edge. Fold rectangle in half lengthwise to cover filling. Seal dough edges with the edge of a plate. With a pizza cutter, cut dough into 24 strips, about ¾-inch wide. Twist each strip twice and place strips 1 inch apart on prepared baking sheets. Cover and let rise until doubled in bulk, about 30 to 40 minutes. Preheat oven to 375°F (190°C). Bake 10 to 12 minutes, until golden brown. Prepare Powdered Sugar Glaze, and brush on while rolls are still warm. Makes about 24 twists.

Cinnamon Filling:
Combine brown sugar, cinnamon and nuts in a small bowl.

Powdered Sugar Glaze:
Combine powdered sugar, melted butter or margarine and hot water in a small bowl to make a thin glaze.

Super-Duper Doughnuts

The spice is nice!

Cooking oil for frying	¼ teaspoon nutmeg
2 cups QUICK MIX, page 15	1 teaspoon vanilla
	1 egg, well beaten
¼ cup sugar	⅓ cup milk or water
¼ teaspoon cinnamon	Vanilla Glaze, see below

Vanilla Glaze:

1¼ cups powdered sugar	½ teaspoon vanilla
2 teaspoons milk	

In a deep-fryer, heat oil to 375°F (190°C). In a medium bowl, combine QUICK MIX, sugar, cinnamon and nutmeg. Blend well. In a small bowl, mix together vanilla, egg, and milk or water. Add all at once to dry ingredients. Stir until well-blended. On a lightly floured surface, knead dough about 10 minutes. Roll out to ½-inch thickness and cut with a floured doughnut cutter. Fry in hot oil about 1 minute on each side, until golden brown. Drain on paper towels. While doughnuts cool slightly, prepare Vanilla Glaze. Dip warm doughnuts in glaze. Makes about 12 doughnuts.

Vanilla Glaze:

Combine all ingredients and stir until smooth.

Tatonuts

This old-fashioned favorite is easy!

1 tablespoon yeast
½ cup lukewarm water
2 eggs, beaten
½ cup melted butter or margarine
3 tablespoons sugar
½ cup instant potato flakes

1 cup milk, scalded
4½ to 5 cups HOT ROLL MIX, page 17
Vegetable oil for frying
Vanilla Glaze, see page 71

Lightly grease 2 baking sheets. In a large bowl, dissolve yeast in lukewarm water. Stir in eggs and butter or margarine. Add sugar, potato flakes and milk. Blend well. Add 4½ cups HOT ROLL MIX and stir thoroughly. Add additional HOT ROLL MIX to make a soft, but not too sticky dough. Turn out on a lightly floured surface. Knead about 5 minutes until dough is smooth and satiny. Lightly butter bowl. Put dough in bowl and turn to butter top. Cover dough with a damp towel and let rise in a warm place until doubled in bulk, about 1 hour. Punch down. On a lightly floured surface, roll out dough about ¼-inch thick. Cut with a floured doughnut cutter. Place on prepared baking sheets. Cover and let rise until doubled in bulk, about 30 to 40 minutes. In a deep-fryer or electric skillet, heat ½ inch of oil to 375°F (190°C). Fry doughnuts about 1 minute on each side, until golden brown. Drain on paper towels. While still warm, brush doughnuts with Vanilla Glaze. Makes about 30 doughnuts.

Cinnamon Rolls

The family's favorite. Watch them disappear!

1 tablespoon active dry yeast	5 to 6 cups HOT ROLL MIX, page 17
1½ cups lukewarm water	Cinnamon Sprinkle, see below
2 eggs, beaten	Sweet Glaze, see below
½ cup vegetable oil or melted margarine	

Cinnamon Sprinkle:

2 tablespoons butter or margarine	1½ teaspoons cinnamon
½ cup brown sugar	½ cup raisins
	¼ cup chopped nuts

Sweet Glaze:

1 cup sifted powdered sugar	¼ teaspoon vanilla
	About 2 tablespoons milk

In a large bowl, dissolve yeast in lukewarm water. Blend in eggs and oil or margarine. Add 5 cups of HOT ROLL MIX. Stir well. Add additional HOT ROLL MIX to make a soft, but not too sticky dough. Knead about 5 minutes until dough is smooth. Lightly butter bowl. Put dough in bowl and turn to butter top. Cover dough with a damp towel and let rise in a warm place until doubled in bulk, about 1 hour. Generously grease 2 baking sheets. Prepare Cinnamon Sprinkle. Punch down dough. Let stand 10 minutes. On a lightly floured surface, roll out dough to a 12″ × 24″ rectangle, about ¼-inch thick. Spread generously with Cinnamon Sprinkle. Roll dough like a jelly roll and cut with a sharp knife into twenty-four 1-inch slices. Place on prepared baking sheets. Cover with a damp towel and let rise in a warm place until doubled in bulk, about 30 to 60 minutes. Preheat oven to 375°F (190°C). Bake 20 to 25 minutes, until golden brown. Prepare Sweet Glaze, and brush on while rolls are still warm. Makes about 24 rolls.

Cinnamon Sprinkle:

Melt butter or margarine in a small saucepan. Stir in brown sugar, cinnamon, raisins and nuts.

Sweet Glaze:

In a small bowl combine powdered sugar, vanilla and enough milk to make a thin mixture.

Cream Cheese Swirls

A real bake shop treat.

1 tablespoon active dry yeast	5 to 6 cups HOT ROLL MIX, page 17
1½ cups lukewarm water	Sugar-Cinnamon Sprinkle,
2 eggs, beaten	see below
½ cup vegetable oil or melted margarine	Sweet Glaze, see below

Sugar-Cinnamon Sprinkle:

2 tablespoons butter or margarine, melted	1½ teaspoons cinnamon
½ cup brown sugar, firmly packed	

Cream Cheese Filling:

1 (8-oz.) pkg. cream cheese, softened	1 egg, slightly beaten
6 tablespoons sugar	½ teaspoon vanilla

Sweet Glaze:

1 cup sifted powdered sugar	¼ teaspoon vanilla
	About 2 tablespoons milk

In a large bowl, dissolve yeast in lukewarm water. Blend in eggs and oil or margarine. Add 5 cups of HOT ROLL MIX. Stir well. Add additional HOT ROLL MIX to make a soft, but not too sticky dough. Knead about 5 minutes until dough is smooth. Lightly butter bowl. Put dough in bowl and turn to butter top. Cover dough with a damp towel and let rise in a warm place until doubled in bulk, about 1 hour. Generously grease 2 baking sheets. Prepare Sugar-Cinnamon Sprinkle and Cream Cheese Filling. Punch down dough. Let stand 10 minutes. On a lightly floured surface, roll out dough to a 12″ × 24″ rectangle, about ¼-inch thick. Spread generously with Sugar-Cinnamon Sprinkle. Roll dough like a jelly roll. Cut into 1-inch slices. Place on prepared baking sheets. Cover with a damp towel and let rise in a warm place until doubled in bulk, about 30 to 60 minutes. Preheat oven to 375°F (190°C). With a tablespoon, press a deep indentation in the center of each bun. Fill the indentation with 3 tablespoons Cream Cheese Filling. Bake 20 to 25 minutes, until golden brown. Prepare Sweet Glaze. Drizzle glaze on warm buns. Makes about 24 rolls.

Sugar-Cinnamon Sprinkle:

Combine all ingredients in a small bowl.

Cream Cheese Filling:

In a small bowl cream together cream cheese and sugar until smooth. Add eggs and vanilla. Mix well.

Sweet Glaze:

In a small bowl combine powdered sugar, vanilla and enough milk to make a thin mixture.

How to Make Butterscotch Butter Balls

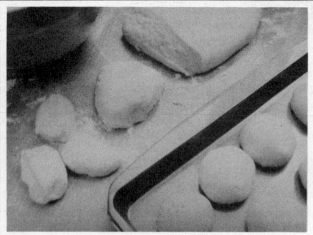

1/Divide the dough into 48 balls and place the balls on cookie sheets. Cover with plastic wrap and freeze.

2/Place 24 frozen balls in each bundt pan. Sprinkle butterscotch pudding over the balls, then pour the mixture of butter or margarine and brown sugar over each pan of rolls.

Butterscotch Butter Balls

A melt-in-your-mouth specialty.

1½ cups lukewarm water
1 tablespoon active dry
  yeast
2 eggs, beaten
½ cup vegetable oil or
  melted margarine
5 to 6 cups HOT ROLL
  MIX, page 17
1 (3-oz.) pkg. regular
  butterscotch pudding

1 cup butter or margarine,
  melted
1 cup brown sugar, firmly
  packed
1 (1½-oz.) pkg. pecans,
  chopped
2 teaspoons cinnamon

In a large bowl, dissolve yeast in lukewarm water.
Blend in eggs and oil or margarine. Add 5 cups of
HOT ROLL MIX. Stir well. Add additional HOT
ROLL MIX to make a soft, but not too sticky dough.
Knead about 5 minutes until dough is smooth. Lightly
butter bowl. Put dough in bowl and turn to butter top.
Cover dough with a damp towel and let rise in a warm
place until doubled in bulk, about 1 hour. Punch down
dough. Divide dough into 48 balls of equal size. Place
balls on a cookie sheet. Cover with plastic wrap and
freeze. When frozen, transfer to plastic bags for storage
in freezer. Use within 1 to 2 months. About 8 hours
before serving, or the night before, place 24 frozen
balls in each of 2 unbuttered bundt pans. Sprinkle half
of butterscotch pudding on each pan of frozen rolls.
Combine melted butter or margarine and brown sugar
in a small bowl. Pour half of mixture over each pan of
rolls. Sprinkle half of pecans and half of cinnamon over
each pan. Cover both pans with towels and let rise
about 8 hours or overnight. Preheat oven to 350°F
(175°C). Bake about 30 minutes, until golden brown.
Makes 2 butterscotch rings.

Pluckit

A fun pull-apart bread for snack or mealtime.

1 tablespoon active dry
  yeast
1½ cups lukewarm water
2 eggs, beaten
½ cup vegetable oil or
  melted margarine

5 to 6 cups HOT ROLL
  MIX, page 17
3 teaspoons cinnamon
¾ cup sugar
½ cup butter or marga-
  rine, melted

In a large bowl, dissolve yeast in lukewarm water.
Blend in eggs and oil or margarine. Add 5 cups of
HOT ROLL MIX. Stir well. Add additional HOT
ROLL MIX to make a soft, but not too sticky dough.
Knead about 5 minutes until dough is smooth. Lightly
butter bowl. Put dough in bowl and turn to butter top.
Cover dough with a damp towel and let rise in a warm
place until doubled in bulk, about 1 hour. Punch down
dough. Roll dough into balls about the size of a walnut. Combine cinnamon and sugar in a small bowl.
Dip balls in melted butter or margarine and roll in
cinnamon-sugar mixture. Pile loosely into an unbuttered tube pan. Let rise until doubled in bulk, about 30
minutes. Preheat oven to 400°F (205°C). Bake about
10 minutes. Lower temperature to 350°F (175°C) and
continue baking 30 minutes until golden. Loosen edges
with a knife and turn out onto a plate. Rolls can be
plucked off one at a time. Makes 1 large pan of rolls.

Variation

To make a coffee cake, roll the balls of dough in
cinnamon-sugar mixture, then in ½ cup chopped nuts.

Quick Wheat Breakfast Cake

*Serve this cinnamon-nut tidbit
on a cold winter morning!*

1 egg, slightly beaten
¾ cup water
2¼ cups WHEAT MIX,
   page 20
1 cup chopped raisins

½ cup brown sugar,
   firmly packed
2 teaspoons cinnamon
½ cup chopped nuts

Preheat oven to 375°F (190°C). Butter an 8-inch square pan. Combine egg and water in a medium bowl. Stir in WHEAT MIX and raisins until moistened. Spread into prepared pan. Combine brown sugar, cinnamon and nuts in a small bowl. Sprinkle on top of cake. Bake 25 to 30 minutes until a toothpick inserted in center comes out clean. Cut into 2-inch squares and serve warm. Makes 16 squares.

Variation
Substitute orange peel and orange juice for part of the water in the recipe.

Sunshine Coffeecake

*A moist muffin-textured cake—
with a variety of toppings.*

3 cups QUICK MIX,
   page 15
⅓ cup sugar
1 egg, slightly beaten

1 cup milk or water
1 teaspoon vanilla
Cinnamon Crumble
   Topping, see below

Cinnamon Crumble Topping:

⅓ cup all-purpose flour
½ cup dry breadcrumbs
   or cookie or cake
   crumbs
½ cup brown sugar,
   firmly packed

1 teaspoon cinnamon
¼ cup butter or
   margarine

Preheat oven to 350°F (175°C). Butter an 8-inch square pan. In a medium bowl, combine QUICK MIX and sugar until evenly distributed. In a small bowl, combine egg, milk or water, and vanilla. Stir until just blended. Add liquid ingredients all at once to dry ingredients. Fold mixture together until blended. Prepare Cinnamon Crumble Topping. Spread half the batter in the prepared pan. Spread half of topping over the batter. Top with remaining batter and topping. Bake 40 to 50 minutes. Makes one 8-inch cake.

Cinnamon Crumble Topping:
In a medium bowl combine flour, crumbs, brown sugar and cinnamon. With a pastry blender, cut in butter or margarine until mixture is crumbly.

Variations
Fruit Crumble Topping: Prepare 1½ cups sweetened sliced, fresh or frozen fruit. Spread over first half of batter and top with Cinnamon Crumble Topping, see above. Proceed according to recipe directions.
Apple Crumble Topping: Add 1½ cups peeled, finely chopped apples and ½ cup raisins to Cinnamon Crumble Topping, see above. Spread mixture on top of coffee cake before baking for a crusty topping, or on bottom of pan for a moist coffee cake.
Date-Nut Topping: Omit Cinnamon Crumble Topping. In a small bowl, combine 1 cup brown sugar and ¼ cup all-purpose flour until well-blended. In another bowl, mix together ½ cup chopped pitted dates and 1 teaspoon vanilla; add to brown sugar mixture. Stir in ½ cup chopped nuts. Cut in ¼ cup butter or margarine until mixture is crumbly. Proceed according to recipe directions.
Chocolate Swirl Topping: Omit Cinnamon Crumble Topping. Melt ⅓ cup semisweet chocolate chips in a small saucepan. In a small bowl, combine ⅓ cup flaked coconut, ¼ cup chopped nuts, ¼ cup sugar and 1 tablespoon melted butter or margarine. Pour coffee cake batter into prepared pan. Spoon melted chocolate

over batter. With a knife, cut through batter several times for a marbled effect. Sprinkle coconut mixture evenly over the top, and bake as directed above.

Mary's Honey-Walnut Swirl

The compliments will be as sweet as the bread!

2 tablespoons active dry yeast	1 teaspoon orange peel
1 cup lukewarm water	1 teaspoon lemon peel
2 eggs, beaten	6½ to 7 cups HOT ROLL MIX, page 17
1 cup water	Honey Filling, see below
4 tablespoons vegetable oil	Powdered Sugar Glaze, pages 70–71

Honey Filling:

¾ cup sugar	1 teaspoon cinnamon
¼ cup honey	¼ teaspoon salt
1 egg, beaten	½ cup chopped nuts
½ teaspoon vanilla	

In a large bowl, dissolve yeast in 1 cup lukewarm water. When yeast starts to bubble, add eggs, 1 cup water, oil, orange peel and lemon peel. Blend well. Add HOT ROLL MIX 1 cup at a time to make a soft dough. On a lightly floured surface, knead dough 5 to 7 minutes, until smooth and satiny. Lightly butter bowl. Put dough in bowl and turn to butter top. Cover with a damp towel and let rise in a warm place until doubled in bulk, about 1 hour. Punch down dough. Prepare Honey Filling. Preheat oven to 375°F (190°C). Butter two 9″ × 5″ loaf pans. Divide dough into 2 balls. Roll out each ball to two 9″ × 14″ rectangles, about ½-inch thick. Spread Honey Filling to within 1 inch of edges. Roll up like a jelly roll from small end, lifting dough slightly and sealing edges as you roll. Seal ends and put into prepared pans, seam-side down. Cover and let rise in a warm place until dough is slightly rounded above top of pan. Bake 45 to 50 minutes, until deep golden brown. Cool on a wire rack. While still warm, drizzle Powdered Sugar Glaze on top of loaves. Makes 2 loaves.

Honey Filling:
Combine all ingredients in a small bowl. Blend well.

> *To slice rolled dough with heavy-duty thread instead of a knife, place the thread crosswise under the roll, pull the ends up and cross them over the roll.*

How to Make Mary's Honey-Walnut Swirl

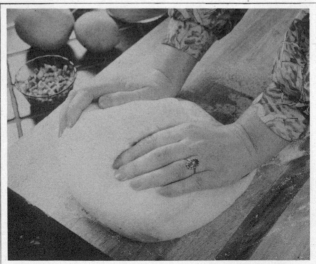

1/On a lightly floured surface, knead the yeast dough
5 to 7 minutes until smooth and satiny.

2/Spread the filling to within 1 inch
of the edges of the dough rectangles.
Then roll the dough like a jelly roll.

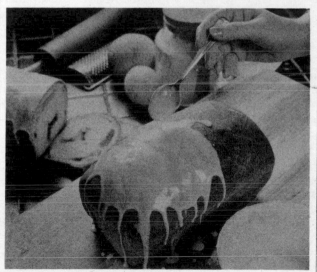

3/While the baked loaves are still warm,
drizzle glaze over the top of each.

Madeline's Muffins

Sweet and moist with a golden-brown pebbly top.

2½ cups QUICK   1 cup milk or water
  MIX, page 15   Butter and honey, if
4 tablespoons sugar   desired
1 egg, beaten

Preheat oven to 425°F (220°C). Generously butter muffin pans. Place QUICK MIX in a medium bowl. Add sugar and mix well. In a small bowl, combine egg and milk or water. Add all at once to dry ingredients. Stir until just blended. Fill prepared muffin pans ⅔ full. Bake 15 to 20 minutes, until golden brown. Serve hot with butter and honey, if desired. Makes 12 large muffins.

Variations

Raisin, Date or Nut Muffins: Add ½ cup finely chopped raisins, dates or nuts to dry ingredients before adding liquid ingredients. Before baking, sprinkle generously with mixture of cinnamon and sugar.

Blueberry Muffins: Add 1 cup well-drained blueberries to dry ingredients before adding liquid ingredients.

Oatmeal or Bran Muffins. Reduce QUICK MIX to 1¾ cups. Add ¾ cup quick rolled oats or all-bran cereal to dry ingredients before adding liquid ingredients.

Cheese Muffins: Add ½ to ¾ cup grated Cheddar cheese to dry ingredients before adding liquid ingredients.

Brown Sugar Muffins: Substitute brown sugar for granulated sugar.

Bacon Bits Muffins: Add 4 strips of cooked, crumbled bacon to dry ingredients before adding liquid ingredients.

Apple Muffins: Add 1 cup grated raw apple to dry ingredients before adding liquid ingredients and increase baking time to 20 to 25 minutes.

Orange Muffins: Add 1 tablespoon fresh orange peel or 1½ teaspoons dehydrated orange peel to dry ingredients before adding liquid ingredients.

Cranberry Muffins: Add ⅔ cup chopped cranberries to dry ingredients before adding liquid ingredients.

Oatmeal Muffins

A sweet, nutty flavor!

1 egg	3 cups OATMEAL MIX,
⅔ cup milk	pages 18–19

Preheat oven to 400°F (205°C). Generously butter muffin pans. Put OATMEAL MIX in a medium bowl. Combine egg and milk in a small bowl. Add all at once to OATMEAL MIX. Stir until just moistened; batter should be lumpy. Fill prepared muffin pans ⅔ full. Bake 15 to 20 minutes until golden brown. Makes 12 large muffins.

Melt-In-Your-Mouth Muffins

A delicious addition to bacon and eggs.

2⅓ cups MUFFIN MIX,	1 egg, beaten
page 18	1 cup milk

Preheat oven to 400°F (205°C). Butter muffin pans. Put MUFFIN MIX in a medium bowl. Combine egg and milk in a small bowl. Add all at once to MUFFIN MIX. Stir until mix is just moistened; batter should be lumpy. Fill prepared muffin pans ⅔ full. Bake 15 to 20 minutes, until golden brown. Makes 12 large muffins.

Variations

Jelly Muffins: Fill each muffin cup ⅓ full with batter. Drop 1 teaspoon jelly on top of batter. Fill cups ⅔ full of batter.

Butterscotch-Pecan Muffins: Melt 6 tablespoons butter or margarine in a small saucepan. Stir in 6 tablespoons brown sugar. Place 1 tablespoon of brown sugar mixture and 2 to 3 pecans in bottom of each muffin cup. Fill cups ⅔ full with batter.

Cheese Muffins: Add 1 cup grated Cheddar cheese to MUFFIN MIX before adding liquid ingredients.

Pineapple Muffins: Decrease milk to ⅔ cup. Add 1 cup crushed pineapple with juice to liquid ingredients before adding liquid to MUFFIN MIX.

Apricot Muffins: Add 1 cup chopped dried apricots to liquid ingredients before adding liquid to MUFFIN MIX.

Banana Muffins: Add ¼ teaspoon cinnamon and ¼ teaspoon nutmeg to MUFFIN MIX. Mash 1 banana and add to liquid ingredients before adding liquid to MUFFIN MIX.

Blueberry Muffins: Add 1 cup well-drained blueberries to liquid ingredients before adding liquid to MUFFIN MIX.

Apple Muffins

The best way to have an apple a day.

2⅓ cups MUFFIN MIX, page 18	1 cup sweet applesauce
½ cup chopped nuts	¼ cup milk
¼ teaspoon cloves	1 egg, beaten

Preheat oven to 400°F (205°C). Butter muffin pans. In a medium bowl, combine MUFFIN MIX, nuts and cloves. Combine applesauce, milk and egg in a small bowl. Add all at once to dry ingredients. Stir until just moistened; batter should be lumpy. Fill prepared muffin pans ⅔ full. Bake 15 to 20 minutes until golden brown. Makes 12 large muffins.

Molasses-Bran Muffins

Did you know molasses is rich in iron?

1 cup bran cereal	1 egg
¾ cup milk	1¼ cups MUFFIN MIX,
2 tablespoons molasses	page 18

Preheat oven to 400°F (205°C). Butter muffin pans. In a small bowl combine bran and milk. Combine molasses and egg in another small bowl. Stir into bran mixture. Put MUFFIN MIX in a medium bowl. Add bran-molasses mixture all at once to MUFFIN MIX. Stir until just moistened; batter should be lumpy. Fill prepared muffin pans ⅔ full. Bake 15 to 20 minutes, until golden brown. Makes 12 large muffins.

Variation

Add 1 cup raisins or chopped dates to bran mixture.

Cornmeal Muffins

You only add 2 ingredients!

2½ cups CORNMEAL	1 egg
MIX, pages 17–18	1¼ cups milk

Preheat oven to 425°F (220°C). Butter muffin pans. Put CORNMEAL MIX in a medium bowl. Combine egg and milk in a small bowl. Add all at once to CORNMEAL MIX. Blend. Fill prepared muffin pans ⅔ full. Bake 15 to 20 minutes, until golden brown. Makes 12 large muffins.

Variations

Surprise Muffins: Fill prepared muffin cups ⅓ full of cornbread batter. Put 1 teaspoon of jam or jelly on top of batter. Spoon additional batter on top of jam or jelly to fill ⅔ full.

Pineapple Corn Muffins: Substitute ¾ cup pineapple juice and ½ cup water for milk in recipe. Stir ½ cup drained crushed pineapple into batter.

Brunch Muffins: Gently fold 6 slices cooked crumbled bacon into batter.

Cornbread: Butter an 8-inch square pan. Spread batter in pan, and bake about 25 minutes, until golden brown.

Gruffins

Introducing a new kind of
crunch and a refreshing flavor.

¾ cup all-purpose flour
¾ cup whole-wheat flour
½ teaspoon salt
4 teaspoons baking
  powder
1 cup GRANOLA MIX,
  pages 33–34

½ cup brown sugar,
  firmly packed
2 eggs, beaten
1 cup milk
⅓ cup vegetable oil

Preheat oven to 425°F (220°C). Generously butter muffin pans. In a large bowl, combine all-purpose flour, whole-wheat flour, salt and baking powder. Add GRANOLA MIX and brown sugar. Stir well. In a small bowl, combine egg, milk and oil. Add all at once to dry ingredients. Stir until just moistened; batter should be lumpy. Fill prepared muffin pans ⅔ full. Bake 15 to 20 minutes, until golden brown. Makes 12 large muffins.

Quick Wheat Muffins

Serve hot. How yummy!

3 cups WHEAT MIX,
  page 20
2 tablespoons sugar

1 egg, slightly beaten
1 cup water

Preheat oven to 400°F (205°C). Generously butter muffin pans. In a medium bowl, combine WHEAT MIX and sugar. Blend well. Combine egg and water in a small bowl. Add all at once to dry ingredients. Stir until just moistened; batter should be lumpy. Fill prepared muffin pans ⅔ full. Bake 15 to 20 minutes, until golden brown. Makes 12 large muffins.

Whole-Wheat Muffins

Family members won't need coaxing
to eat these delights.

⅔ cup whole-wheat flour
1½ cups MUFFIN MIX,
   page 18

1 egg, beaten
1 cup milk

Preheat oven to 400°F (205°C). Butter muffin pans. In a medium bowl, combine whole-wheat flour and MUFFIN MIX. Combine egg and milk in a small bowl. Add all at once to dry ingredients. Stir until just moistened; batter should be lumpy. Fill prepared muffin pans ⅔ full. Bake 15 to 20 minutes, until golden brown. Makes 12 large muffins.

Puff Oven Pancakes

Makes a spectacular entrance whenever served.

4 tablespoons butter or
   margarine
4 eggs
⅔ cup milk

⅔ cup PANCAKE MIX,
   page 19
Fiesta Fruit Topping,
   see below

Fiesta Fruit Topping:

1 (10-oz.) pkg. frozen
   raspberries or straw-
   berries, thawed
1 cup pineapple chunks,
   drained

1 banana, sliced
¼ cup brown sugar,
   firmly packed
¼ cup sour cream

Preheat oven to 450°F (230°C). Put 2 tablespoons butter or margarine each in two 9-inch pie plates. Put in preheating oven to melt butter or margarine. In a blender, combine eggs, milk and PANCAKE MIX. Pour batter into pie plates. Bake about 18 minutes, until pancakes are puffy and browned. Do not open oven while pancakes are cooking. Top with Fiesta Fruit Topping or your choice of topping. Makes 2 large pancakes.

Fiesta Fruit Topping:

Spoon raspberries or strawberries on top of each warm Puff Oven Pancake. Top with pineapple chunks and banana. Sprinkle brown sugar over top. Top with teaspoonfuls of sour cream. Serve immediately.

Variation

Tart Lemon Topping: Sprinkle 1½ teaspoons lemon juice over top of each warm Puff Oven Pancake. Sprinkle powdered sugar over top. Serve immediately.

Perfect Pancakes

For variety, add your favorite fruit to the batter.

1½ cups PANCAKE MIX,   1 cup water
    page 19   3 tablespoons vegetable
1 egg, slightly beaten   oil

Put PANCAKE MIX in a medium bowl. Combine egg, water and oil in a small bowl. Add egg mixture to PANCAKE MIX. Add more water for thinner pancakes. Blend well. Let stand 5 minutes. Cook on a hot oiled griddle about 3 to 4 minutes, until browned on both sides. Makes ten to twelve 4-inch pancakes.

Variation

Onion Rings: Preheat oil in deep-fryer to 375°F (190°C). Make pancake batter with ice water. Dip thinly sliced, separated onion rings into batter, then fry about 2 minutes, until golden.

Oat Pancakes

Add this to your list of early morning favorites.

1½ cups OATMEAL MIX, pages 18–19	1 cup water 1 egg, slightly beaten

In a medium bowl, combine OATMEAL MIX, water and egg. Blend well. Let stand 5 minutes. Cook on a hot oiled griddle about 3 to 4 minutes, until browned on both sides. Makes twelve to fifteen 4-inch pancakes.

Favorite Wheat Pancakes

Extra easy and especially nourishing.

1 egg, slightly beaten 1½ cups water	2¼ cups WHEAT MIX, page 20

Combine egg and water in a medium bowl. Stir in WHEAT MIX until just moistened. Cook on a hot oiled griddle about 3 to 4 minutes, until browned on both sides. Makes about fifteen 4-inch pancakes.

Wheat Waffles

Make these often with a variety of toppings.

2¼ cups WHEAT MIX, page 20 1⅓ cups water	3 tablespoons vegetable oil 3 eggs, separated

Preheat waffle baker. In a large bowl, combine WHEAT MIX, water, oil and egg yolks. Beat until just blended. In a medium glass or metal bowl, beat egg whites until stiff. Fold into wheat mixture. Bake according to waffle baker instructions. Makes 3 or 4 large waffles.

Nevada's Pancakes

Light, crisp and brown outside,
moist and tender inside.

2¼ cups **QUICK MIX**,　　1 egg, beaten
　　page 15　　　　　　　　1½ cups milk or water
1 tablespoon sugar

Combine QUICK MIX and sugar in a medium bowl.
Mix well. Combine egg and milk or water in a small
bowl. Add all at once to dry ingredients. Blend well.
Let stand 5 to 10 minutes. Cook on a hot oiled griddle
about 3 to 4 minutes, until browned on both sides.
Makes ten to twelve 4-inch pancakes.

Variation

Nevada's Waffles: Bake batter in oiled preheated waffle
baker until golden brown. Makes 3 large waffles.

Golden French Toast

Dipped in a better batter.

2 eggs, beaten　　　　　　10 slices bread
1 cup milk　　　　　　　　Butter for grill
1 cup **PANCAKE MIX**,
　　page 19

In a medium, shallow bowl, combine eggs, milk and
PANCAKE MIX. Blend well. Dip bread slices into the
batter and cook on a hot, buttered griddle about 3 to
4 minutes, until lightly browned on both sides. Makes
10 slices of French Toast.

> *Muffins are better in quality if you butter the*
> *muffin pans rather than use cupcake liners.*

BREADS & ROLLS

People often think breads are difficult to make: quick breads aren't quick enough and yeast breads are a scary process! But they're all so easy and delicious when you make them with your own mixes.

Let QUICK MIX work wonders on those quick breads you don't have time to make the old way. Make Banana-Nut Bread and Spice-Nut Bread the same hour. After you make Golden Cornbread, turn back to the Breakfast & Brunch chapter for variations with Cornmeal Muffins, and keep baking!

Since quick breads are similar to muffins in the proportion of liquid to dry ingredients, be careful not to overbeat them. Stir the batter briskly about 30 seconds and let your oven complete the preparation process.

Did you know biscuits are lighter if the gluten in them is developed a little? You do this by kneading the dough 10 to 15 times. Your biscuits will rise higher and you'll wish you had always made them this way.

HOT ROLL MIX makes it easier for both the beginner and the expert cook to create a wonderful variety of homebaked yeast breads and rolls. You will enjoy working with this dough. It is soft, elastic and easy to handle. The aroma and fine texture of your baked products will delight everyone—especially you. Begin with Homemade White Bread, and promise yourself you'll try every recipe. The hot rolls come in several shapes you can make all at once. Spread your fresh hot breads and rolls with Honey Butter, page 100.

Now do you feel like the master of your kitchen? Good—treat yourself to some Big Soft Pretzels!

Pan Rolls

Quick, easy and old-fashioned.

1 tablespoon active dry yeast	½ cup vegetable oil or melted margarine
1½ cups lukewarm water	5 to 6 cups HOT ROLL MIX, page 17
2 eggs, beaten	

In a large bowl, dissolve yeast in lukewarm water. Blend in eggs and oil or margarine. Add 5 cups HOT ROLL MIX. Blend well. Add additional HOT ROLL MIX to make a soft, but not too sticky dough. Knead about 5 minutes until dough is smooth. Lightly butter bowl. Put dough in bowl and turn to butter top. Cover dough with a damp towel and let rise in a warm place until doubled in bulk, about 1 hour. Grease a 13" × 9" baking pan or two 9-inch, round pans. Punch down dough. Divide dough into 24 to 30 balls of equal size. Place balls in prepared pans. Cover and let rise again until doubled in bulk, about 30 to 40 minutes. Preheat oven to 375°F (190°C). Bake 20 to 25 minutes, until golden brown. Makes about 24 rolls.

Crescent Rolls

Buttery, rich and golden.

1 tablespoon active dry yeast	5 to 6 cups HOT ROLL MIX, page 17
1½ cups lukewarm water	2 tablespoons butter or margarine, softened
2 eggs, beaten	
½ cup vegetable oil or melted margarine	

In a large bowl, dissolve yeast in lukewarm water. Blend in eggs and oil or margarine. Add 5 cups HOT ROLL MIX. Blend well. Add additional HOT ROLL MIX to make a soft, but not too sticky dough. Knead about 5 minutes until dough is smooth. Lightly butter bowl. Put dough in bowl and turn to butter top. Cover dough with a damp towel and let rise in a warm place until doubled in bulk, about 1 hour. Generously grease baking sheets. Punch down dough. Divide in half. Let stand 10 minutes. On a lightly floured surface, roll out each half to a 12-inch circle. Brush each circle with 1 tablespoon soft butter or margarine. Cut each circle into 16 pie-shaped wedges. Roll up each wedge from the wide end. Place point-side down in a crescent shape on prepared baking sheets. Cover and let rise again until doubled in bulk, about 45 to 60 minutes. Preheat oven to 400°F (205°C). Bake 15 to 20 minutes, until golden brown. Makes about 32 rolls.

Orange Butterflake Rolls

A touch of citrus adds a delightful taste!

1 tablespoon active dry yeast	5 to 6 cups HOT ROLL MIX, page 17
1½ cups lukewarm water	Orange Butter, see below
2 eggs, beaten	Orange Glaze, see below
½ cup vegetable oil or melted margarine	

Orange Butter:

2 tablespoons butter or margarine, melted	2 tablespoons grated orange peel
½ cup sugar	

Orange Glaze:

1 cup sifted powdered sugar	About 2 tablespoons orange juice

In a large bowl, dissolve yeast in lukewarm water. Blend in eggs and oil or margarine. Add 5 cups HOT ROLL MIX. Blend well. Add additional HOT ROLL MIX to make a soft, but not too sticky dough. Knead about 5 minutes until dough is smooth. Lightly butter bowl. Put dough in bowl and turn to butter top. Cover dough with a damp towel and let rise in a warm place until doubled in bulk, about 1 hour. Generously grease muffin pans. Prepare Orange Butter. Punch down dough. Let stand 10 minutes. On a lightly floured surface, roll out dough to a 10″ × 20″ rectangle. Brush with Orange Butter. Cut into twenty 1″ × 10″ strips. Stack 5 strips together. Cut each stack into 6 equal pieces. Place each cut stack upright in prepared muffin pans. Cover and let rise again until doubled in bulk, about 30 minutes. Preheat oven to 400°F (205°C). Bake 15 to 20 minutes, until golden brown. Prepare Orange Glaze, and brush on while rolls are still warm. Makes about 24 rolls.

Orange Butter:
Combine butter, sugar and orange peel.

Orange Glaze:
Blend powdered sugar and orange juice until smooth.

> *Yeast doughs are doubled in bulk when an indentation made with your finger remains in the dough.*

Indian Fry Bread

Serve it hot with Honey Butter,
page 100, or refried beans.

Vegetable oil for frying
1 cup QUICK MIX,
  page 15
½ cup flour

¼ teaspoon salt
About ⅓ cup milk or
  water

In a deep skillet, heat oil to 375°F (190°C). In a medium bowl, combine QUICK MIX, flour and salt. Mix well. Add enough milk or water to make a soft dough. On a lightly floured surface, knead about 12 times. Divide into two balls. Pat or roll each ball out to ¼-inch thickness. Cut into 6 wedges. Fry in hot oil about 2 to 3 minutes until brown on both sides. Drain on paper towels. Makes 12 wedges.

Homemade White Bread

This will remind you of Grandma's
homemade bread, but you'll make it faster.

2 tablespoons active dry
  yeast
1 cup lukewarm water
2 eggs, beaten
1 cup water

4 tablespoons vegetable
  oil
6½ to 7 cups HOT
  ROLL MIX, page 17
Butter or margarine

In a large bowl, dissolve yeast in lukewarm water. When yeast starts to bubble, add eggs, water and oil. Blend well. Add HOT ROLL MIX 1 cup at a time, until dough is stiff. On a lightly floured surface, knead dough 5 to 7 minutes, until smooth and satiny. Lightly butter bowl. Put dough in bowl and turn to butter top. Cover with a damp towel and let rise in a warm place until doubled in bulk, about 45 to 60 minutes. Punch down dough. Let stand 10 minutes. Shape into 2 loaves. Grease two 9″ × 5″ loaf pans. Place 1 loaf of dough in each pan, seam-side down. Cover and let rise again until slightly rounded above top of pan, about 30 to 40 minutes. Preheat oven to 375°F (190°C). Bake 45 to 55 minutes, until deep golden brown. Remove from oven and brush tops with butter or margarine. Remove from pans and cool on a wire rack. Makes 2 loaves.

Variation

Raisin Bread: Add 1 cup raisins with HOT ROLL MIX. Toast bread, if desired.

Hi-Light Onion Bread

Perfect for patio party or buffet sandwiches.

2 cups water
1 (1¼-oz.) pkg. dry onion soup mix
2 tablespoons active dry yeast
2 eggs, beaten
4 tablespoons vegetable oil
6½ to 7 cups HOT ROLL MIX, page 17
Butter or margarine

Bring water to a boil in a small saucepan. Add dry soup mix and simmer 10 minutes. Pour into a large bowl and cool to lukewarm. Sprinkle yeast over mixture and stir to dissolve. Add eggs and oil. Beat well. Add HOT ROLL MIX 1 cup at a time, until dough is stiff. On a lightly floured surface, knead dough 5 to 7 minutes, until smooth and satiny. Lightly butter bowl. Put dough in bowl and turn to butter top. Cover with a damp towel and let rise in a warm place until doubled in bulk, about 45 to 60 minutes. Punch down dough. Let stand 10 minutes. Shape into 2 loaves. Grease two 9″ × 5″ loaf pans. Place 1 loaf of dough in each pan, seam-side down. Cover and let rise again until slightly rounded above top of pan, about 30 to 40 minutes. Preheat oven to 375°F (190°C). Bake 45 to 55 minutes, until deep golden brown. Remove from oven and brush tops with butter or margarine. Remove from pans and cool on a wire rack. Makes 2 loaves.

Good-For-You Bread

A nutritious bread full of B vitamins from wheat germ.

2 tablespoons active dry
  yeast
1 cup lukewarm water
2 eggs, beaten
1 cup water
4 tablespoons vegetable
  oil

4 tablespoons brown
  sugar
⅔ cup wheat germ
6½ to 7 cups HOT
  ROLL MIX, page 17
Butter or margarine

In a large bowl, dissolve yeast in lukewarm water. When yeast starts to bubble, add eggs, water and oil. Blend well. Add brown sugar and wheat germ. Blend well. Add HOT ROLL MIX 1 cup at a time, until dough is stiff. On a lightly floured surface, knead dough 5 to 7 minutes, until smooth and satiny. Lightly butter bowl. Put dough in bowl and turn to butter top. Cover with a damp towel and let rise in a warm place until doubled in bulk, about 45 to 60 minutes. Punch down dough. Let stand 10 minutes. Shape into 2 loaves. Grease two 9″ × 5″ loaf pans. Place 1 loaf of dough in each pan, seam-side down. Cover and let rise again until slightly rounded above top of pan, about 30 to 40 minutes. Preheat oven to 375°F (190°C). Bake 45 to 55 minutes, until deep golden brown. Remove from oven and brush tops with butter or margarine. Remove from pans and cool on a wire rack. Makes 2 loaves.

Coffeetime Quick Bread

Delicious toasted and served for breakfast.

1 egg, slightly beaten
1¼ cups water

4 cups WHEAT MIX,
  page 20

Preheat oven to 350°F (175°C). Grease a 9″ × 5″ loaf pan. Combine egg and water in a large bowl. Stir in WHEAT MIX until moistened. Turn into prepared pan and bake about 50 minutes, until a toothpick inserted in center comes out clean. Top of loaf should crack. Cool pan on a wire rack about 5 minutes. Loosen sides of bread with a knife and turn right-side up on wire rack. Cool completely before slicing. Makes 1 loaf.

Golden Cornbread

Golden and good, with baked corn flavor.

1½ cups QUICK MIX, page 15	1 egg, slightly beaten
¾ cup yellow cornmeal	1 cup milk or water
4 teaspoons sugar	Honey Butter, see below

Honey Butter:

1 cup butter, softened	1 egg yolk
1¼ cups honey	

Preheat oven to 400°F (205°C) Butter an 8-inch square pan. In a medium bowl, combine QUICK MIX, cornmeal and sugar. Mix well. Combine egg and milk or water in a small bowl. Add half of egg mixture to dry ingredients. Blend well. Add remaining egg mixture and blend well. Spread evenly in prepared pan. Bake 25 to 30 minutes, until golden brown. Cut into 2-inch squares. Serve hot with Honey Butter. Makes 8 to 10 servings.

Honey Butter:

Combine butter, honey and egg yolk in a deep bowl. Beat with electric mixer 10 minutes. Store in refrigerator. Makes about 2½ cups.

Variations

Blueberry Cornbread: Add 1 cup fresh or partially thawed, drained frozen blueberries to cornbread batter. Stir gently to blend.

Cheese Cornbread: Add ⅔ cup grated Cheddar cheese

and ⅔ cup drained whole kernel corn to batter in pan. Stir gently to blend.

Cornbread Muffins: Butter muffin pans. Fill ⅔ full with cornbread batter. Bake 15 to 20 minutes, until golden brown. Makes 10 to 12 muffins.

Dixie Spoon Bread

Real "down home" flavor.

3½ cups milk	2 eggs, separated
2½ cups CORNMEAL MIX, pages 17–18	

Preheat oven to 325°F (165°C). Lightly grease a 1½-quart casserole. Scald 2½ cups of the milk in a small saucepan. Gradually add CORNMEAL MIX, stirring constantly. Continue cooking and stirring until mixture reaches consistency of thick mush. Stir in egg yolks, 1 at a time. Remove from heat. Stir in remaining 1 cup milk. In a glass bowl, beat egg whites until stiff. Fold into cooked mixture. Put into prepared casserole. Bake about 1 hour, until golden brown. Makes 1 pan of spoon bread.

Banana-Nut Bread

Bake a better banana bread than ever before.

2 cups QUICK MIX, page 15	½ cup buttermilk
⅔ cup sugar	1 cup mashed bananas
½ teaspoon baking soda	1 tablespoon lemon juice
2 eggs, well beaten	½ teaspoon vanilla
	½ cup chopped nuts

Preheat oven to 350°F (175°C). Generously grease a 9″ × 5″ loaf pan. Combine QUICK MIX, sugar and baking soda. Mix well. In a small bowl, combine eggs, buttermilk, bananas, lemon juice and vanilla. Blend well. Add banana mixture to dry ingredients. Beat batter well. Add nuts. Pour into prepared loaf pan. Bake about 1 hour, until a toothpick inserted in center comes out clean. Let stand 5 minutes in pan. Remove from pan and cool on a wire rack. Makes 1 loaf.

Spice-Nut Bread

The nutty flavor is delicious, hot or cold.

3 cups QUICK MIX, page 15
½ cup brown sugar, firmly packed
⅓ cup granulated sugar
1 teaspoon cinnamon, if desired
¼ teaspoon cloves
¼ teaspoon nutmeg
¾ cup chopped nuts
1 egg, slightly beaten
1 cup milk or water

Preheat oven to 350°F (175°C). Generously grease a 9″ × 5″ loaf pan. In a large bowl, combine QUICK MIX, brown sugar, granulated sugar, cinnamon, cloves, nutmeg and nuts until blended. Combine egg and milk or water in a small bowl. Add all at once to dry ingredients. Blend. Pour batter into prepared pan. Level top of batter with a spoon. Bake 45 to 50 minutes, until a toothpick inserted in center comes out clean. Let stand 5 to 10 minutes in pan. Remove from pan and cool on a wire rack. Makes 1 loaf.

Big Soft Pretzels

Try these with a cool drink for a great snack.

1 tablespoon active dry yeast
1½ cups lukewarm water
2 eggs, beaten
½ cup vegetable oil or melted margarine
5 to 6 cups HOT ROLL MIX, page 17
1 egg, beaten
About 2 tablespoons coarse salt

Lightly grease 2 large baking sheets. In a large bowl, dissolve yeast in lukewarm water. Blend in 2 eggs and oil or margarine. Add 5 cups HOT ROLL MIX. Stir well. Add additional HOT ROLL MIX to make a soft, but not too sticky dough. Knead about 5 minutes until dough is smooth. Roll pieces of dough into ropes about ½ inch in diameter and 18 to 24 inches long. Form into pretzel shapes. For pretzel sticks, cut dough into 5- to 6-inch lengths. Place on prepared baking sheets. Preheat oven to 425°F (220°C). Brush tops of pretzels with beaten egg and sprinkle with coarse salt. Bake immediately 12 to 15 minutes, until brown and crisp. Makes 12 to 15 large pretzels.

Variation

For a chewier pretzel, drop pretzel-shaped dough into a pan of boiling water. When dough floats to the top of the water, remove it. Preheat oven to 400°F (205°C). Brush with egg and sprinkle with coarse salt. Bake about 30 minutes.

How to Make Big Soft Pretzels

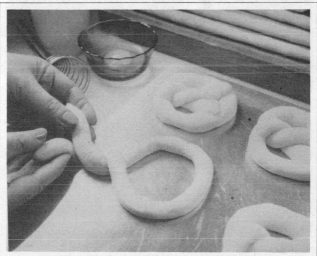

1/Place the ropes of dough on cookie sheets to form a circle and twist the ends twice.

2/Lay the twisted ends of the dough across the circle and press to seal for a traditional pretzel shape.

3/Brush the tops of the pretzels with beaten egg and sprinkle with coarse salt. Bake until brown and crisp.

Crispy Breadsticks

Add crispy crunch to your Italian dishes.

1 cup QUICK MIX,
   page 15
¼ cup cornmeal or all-
   purpose flour
¼ teaspoon salt

About ¼ cup milk or
   water
Sesame or poppy seeds,
   if desired

Preheat oven to 400°F (205°C). Lightly grease a baking sheet. In a medium bowl, combine QUICK MIX, cornmeal or flour, and salt. Add milk or water to form dough. Knead about 12 times, until dough is smooth. Shape into pencil-like strands ½-inch thick. Cut into 8- to 10-inch lengths. Roll in sesame or poppy seeds, if desired. Bake about 20 minutes, until brown and crisp. For extra crispness, turn off oven and leave breadsticks in oven 5 to 10 more minutes. Makes 6 breadsticks.

Karine's Drop Biscuits

When time is short, try this simplified biscuit recipe.

3 cups QUICK MIX,
   page 15

¾ cup milk or water

Preheat oven to 450°F (230°C). Grease a baking sheet. Combine QUICK MIX and milk or water in a medium bowl. Stir until just blended. Drop dough by tablespoonfuls onto prepared baking sheet. Bake 10 to 12 minutes, until golden brown. Makes 12 large drop biscuits.

Variations

Cheese & Herb Biscuits: Add ⅓ cup grated Cheddar cheese and chopped parsley, chives or herbs to taste while stirring dough.

Buttermilk Biscuits: Substitute ¾ cup buttermilk for milk or water.

Country Dumplings: Drop dough by tablespoonfuls over top of boiling beef or chicken stew. Boil gently 10 minutes, uncovered. Cover and cook over medium-high heat 10 more minutes, until cooked through. Makes 12 dumplings.

Orange Biscuits: Add 1 tablespoon grated orange peel. If desired, substitute 2 tablespoons orange juice for part of milk or water.

Fruit Cobbler: Spoon dough over top of hot, sweetened fruit or berries and bake in an 8-inch square pan about 20 to 25 minutes until golden brown.

Never-Fail Rolled Biscuits

These light biscuits separate into layers.

3 cups QUICK MIX,   ⅔ cup milk or water
   page 15

Preheat oven to 450°F (230°C). Combine QUICK MIX and milk or water in a medium bowl. Blend. Let dough stand 5 minutes. On a lightly floured board, knead dough about 15 times. Roll out to ½-inch thickness. Cut with a floured biscuit cutter. Place about 2 inches apart on unbuttered baking sheet. Bake 10 to 12 minutes, until golden brown. Makes 12 large biscuits.

Variations

Cinnamon Rolls: Preheat oven to 400°F (205°C). Roll out dough to a rectangle. Brush with melted butter. Sprinkle with brown sugar and cinnamon. Roll dough like a jelly roll and cut into ½-inch slices. Bake 10 to 15 minutes. Glaze with mixture of powdered sugar and a few drops of water.

Pizza: Use dough as crust for 12 individual pizzas or two 12-inch pizzas. Pat dough to ⅛-inch thickness.

Top with tomato sauce, spices, cheese, meat and choice of toppings.

Meat Pinwheels: Preheat oven to 450°F (230°C). Roll out dough to a rectangle. Chop cooked meat and combine with gravy. Spread over dough. Roll dough like a jelly roll and cut into ½-inch slices. Bake 10 to 12 minutes. Serve with gravy, soup or cheese sauce.

Pot Pie: Use as the top crust of a chicken or meat pot pie.

APPETIZERS & SOUPS

Because appetizers are supposed to be just tasty morsels that tantalize the appetite before a meal, you may not want to spend a long time preparing them when you'd rather visit. Get out your mixes! You can dream up lots of ideas for appetizers as you read through this book. Among the Special Mixes you'll find some delicious chip and vegetable dips. Be sure to try Quick Taco Dip, page 112. Add sour cream to the seasoning mixes to create new dip flavors.

Marie's Fruit Cocktail, page 48, is a refreshing taste for any hot, summer day. So is Fruit Slush, page 47.

You can even make appetizers from MOIST PIE CRUST MIX. Look at Sausage Rolls! If you want your guests to keep coming back for more, Curried Shrimp Rounds and Cocktail Meatballs will make it happen.

Our soups are great "tummy warmers" for the after-the-game crowd. Most can be prepared ahead and reheated in a jiffy.

Use HEARTY SOUP MIX and Hearty Soup Stock for exceptional homemade soups. It's a great way to use leftover vegetables. For a big event, serve Hearty New England Clam Chowder—thick, creamy and rich. A salad and hot bread add the finishing touches to this robust meal.

Learn to master Basic White Sauce easily with WHITE SAUCE MIX. Be creative in preparing your own homemade soups and sauces with it. WHITE

SAUCE MIX is one of the few mixes that require refrigerator storage.

Get into the habit of "appetizing" your guests with a variety of appetizers and soups. Don't forget to use them as snacks, too—even when the only company is you.

Sausage Rolls

Seasoned filling makes these real crowd pleasers.

1 roll MOIST PIE
  CRUST MIX,
  page 40, thawed
1 lb. lean ground pork
  sausage or "hot"
  ground sausage

8 to 10 drops Tabasco®
  sauce
½ teaspoon thyme
¼ teaspoon pepper
2 tablespoons milk

Divide MOIST PIE CRUST MIX dough into 4 balls.
On a lightly floured surface, roll out each ball to a thin
4″ × 12″ rectangle. Preheat oven to 400°F (205°C).
In a small bowl, combine sausage, Tabasco® sauce,
thyme and pepper. Form into 4 rolls, about 12 inches
long. Place a sausage roll lengthwise in the center of
each rectangle. Dampen edges of dough with water.
Roll dough around sausage, pressing securely to seal.
Brush outside of roll with milk. Cut each roll into
six 2-inch lengths. Place on baking sheets, seam-side
down. Cut small slits in crust. Bake about 15 minutes.
Reduce heat to 350°F (175°C) and bake 8 to 10
more minutes. Makes 24 appetizers.

Sausage-Cheese Balls

Guests coming in an hour? This is quick!

1½ cups QUICK MIX,
  page 15
1 lb. grated Cheddar
  cheese

1 lb. lean ground pork
  sausage or "hot"
  ground sausage

Preheat oven to 350°F (175°C). Combine ingredients
until dough sticks together. Roll into 1½-inch balls.
Bake about 25 minutes. Drain on paper towels. Serve
warm on toothpicks. Makes about 75 appetizers.

Cocktail Meatballs

Place this casserole in your
microwave oven and heat it 5 minutes!

2 tablespoons butter
or margarine
⅓ cup chopped green
pepper
⅓ cup chopped onion
1 (10¾-oz.) can con-
densed tomato soup
2 tablespoons brown
sugar, firmly packed

4 teaspoons Worcester-
shire sauce
1 tablespoon prepared
mustard
1 tablespoon vinegar
1 container MEATBALL
MIX, page 24, thawed
(about 30 meatballs)

Preheat oven to 350°F (175°C). Melt butter or margarine in a small saucepan. Sauté green pepper and
onion in butter or margarine until tender. In a 2-quart
casserole, combine tomato soup, brown sugar, Worcestershire sauce, mustard and vinegar. Add sautéed
green pepper and onion. Stir in MEATBALL MIX.
Bake about 20 minutes, until heated through. Keep
warm. Serve meatballs on toothpicks. Makes about 30
appetizers.

Curried Shrimp Rounds

Here's a unique flavor combination you can't resist.

3 cups QUICK MIX,
page 15
⅔ cup milk or water
2 (4½-oz.) cans shrimp,
drained and rinsed
1 cup grated Swiss
cheese
½ cup mayonnaise
2 tablespoons finely
chopped green onion

1 tablespoon lemon juice
¼ teaspoon curry
powder
½ cup thinly sliced
water chestnuts
Parsley flakes, for
garnish

Preheat oven to 400°F (205°C). Grease 2 baking sheets. In a medium bowl, combine QUICK MIX and milk or water. Stir until blended. Let dough stand 5 minutes. On a slightly floured board, knead dough about 15 times. Roll out dough to ⅛-inch thickness. Cut with a small floured cookie cutter and place biscuits on prepared baking sheets. In a small bowl, combine shrimp, Swiss cheese, mayonnaise, onion, lemon juice and curry powder. Spoon shrimp mixture onto biscuits. Top with water chestnuts and sprinkle with parsley. Bake 10 to 12 minutes. Makes about 40 appetizers.

Quick Taco Dip

*Make this a day ahead, then just heat it
and serve with corn chips!*

2 cups READY HAM-
  BURGER MIX,
  page 21, thawed
½ cup "hot" ketchup
1 tablespoon chili
  powder
2 (15½-oz.) cans
  kidney beans

¼ teaspoon Tabasco®
  sauce
1 cup grated Cheddar
  cheese
½ cup chopped green
  olives with pimientos,
  for garnish

In a large saucepan, combine READY HAMBURGER MIX, ketchup and chili powder. Mash kidney beans and add with bean juice to meat mixture. Add Tabasco® sauce. Heat through about 10 minutes. Put in a chafing dish and top with grated Cheddar cheese. Garnish with green olives. Makes about 6 cups dip, enough for 15 to 20 servings.

Basic White Sauce

Acquaint yourself with this family of sauces.

½ cup WHITE SAUCE   Pepper, herbs and spices,
  MIX, page 30   if desired
1 cup cool water

In a small saucepan, combine WHITE SAUCE MIX and water. For thinner sauce, decrease WHITE SAUCE MIX to ¼ cup. For thick sauce, increase WHITE SAUCE MIX to ¾ cup. Cook over low heat until smooth, stirring constantly. Season with pepper, herbs and spices, if desired. Makes about 1½ cups sauce.

Variations

Substitute milk, tomato juice or chicken or beef stock for all or part of water.

Cheese Sauce: Add ½ to 1 cup shredded Cheddar cheese after mixture thickens. Stir until cheese is melted.

Curry Sauce: Add 1 teaspoon curry powder to thickened mixture.

To hard-cook eggs, put the eggs in a small saucepan and cover with water. Bring to a boil. Cover the pan, turn off the burner and let the eggs stand 15 to 20 minutes. Rinse under cold water.

Cream of Chicken Soup

M-m-m-m-m-m-m good!

2 chicken bouillon cubes
2 cups hot water
1½ cups WHITE
   SAUCE MIX, page 30
1 cup minced, cooked
   chicken
½ cup finely chopped
   celery

½ cup finely chopped
   onion
½ teaspoon salt
1 teaspoon garlic salt
4 cups milk
1 egg yolk, beaten
Chopped chives or water-
   cress, for garnish

Dissolve chicken bouillon cubes in hot water. Cool. Combine WHITE SAUCE MIX and bouillon mixture in a large kettle or Dutch oven. Cook over low heat about 5 minutes, stirring constantly, until thick and smooth. Add chicken, celery, onion, salt and garlic salt. Simmer 15 minutes, stirring constantly. Blend in milk and egg yolk. Simmer 5 more minutes. Remove from heat. Garnish with chopped chives or watercress. Makes 6 servings.

Alphabet Vegetable Soup

Special for a chilly day.

3 cups GARDEN
   VEGETABLE MIX,
   page 29, thawed
1 qt. vegetable juice
   cocktail
½ teaspoon seasoned
   pepper

¾ teaspoon salt
⅔ cup alphabet
   macaroni
1 cup pared and cubed
   potatoes

In a large saucepan, combine GARDEN VEGE-TABLE MIX, vegetable juice cocktail, seasoned pepper and salt. Bring to a boil. Add alphabet macaroni and potatoes. Reduce heat to medium. Cook uncovered about 12 to 15 minutes, until macaroni and potatoes are tender. Makes 6 to 8 servings.

Variation

Beef & Vegetable Soup: Brown 1 pound lean ground beef. Drain and add with macaroni and potatoes to soup.

Eastern Corn Chowder

5 slices bacon
1 medium onion, thinly
  sliced
2 medium potatoes,
  pared and diced
Water
2 cups milk
1 cup WHITE SAUCE
  MIX, page 30

1 (17-oz.) can cream-
  style corn
1 teaspoon salt
Dash pepper
1 tablespoon butter or
  margarine, for garnish

In a large frying pan, cook bacon until crisp. Crumble and set aside. Reserve 3 tablespoons bacon drippings in pan. Add onion and cook until light brown. Add potatoes and enough water to cover. Cook over medium heat 10 to 15 minutes, until potatoes are cooked. Combine milk and WHITE SAUCE MIX in a small saucepan. Cook over low heat until thick and smooth, stirring constantly. Stir in cream-style corn, salt and pepper. Add to potato mixture and heat through about 10 minutes. Top each serving with crumbled bacon and butter or margarine. Make 6 servings.

How to Make Eastern Corn Chowder

1/Cook thinly sliced onions in bacon drippings until light brown. Add potatoes and enough water to cover. Cook over medium heat 10 to 15 minutes.

2/Combine 2 cups milk and WHITE SAUCE MIX in a saucepan. Cook until thick and smooth, stirring constantly. Stir in cream-style corn, salt and pepper.

3/Add white sauce and corn mixture to potatoes and heat through.

4/Serve in soup bowls. Top each serving with crumbled bacon.

Hearty New England Clam Chowder

The tantalizing aroma of this chowder says "Welcome home."

2 (6½-oz.) cans minced clams
1 cup finely chopped onions
1 cup finely chopped celery
2 cups pared and diced potatoes
Water
1½ cups WHITE SAUCE MIX, page 30
1 qt. milk
½ teaspoon sugar
Salt and pepper to taste

Drain clams, reserving juice. In a large saucepan, combine clam juice, onions, celery and potatoes. Add enough water to just cover vegetables. Cook over medium heat about 15 minutes until tender. While vegetables are cooking, combine WHITE SAUCE MIX and milk in a large kettle or Dutch oven. Cook over low heat until thick and smooth, stirring constantly. Add clams, undrained vegetables and sugar. Heat through about 15 minutes. Add salt and pepper to taste. Makes 6 servings.

Vegetable-Cheese Soup

*A hearty vegetable combo
with a Mexican touch.*

4 cups boiling water
4 chicken bouillon cubes
2 (16-oz.) cans stewed
  tomatoes
⅛ teaspoon minced garlic
1 tablespoon minced
  onion

2 cups GARDEN
  VEGETABLE MIX,
  page 29, thawed
1 (7-oz.) can green chili
  salsa
¾ lb. grated Monterey
  Jack cheese

In a large kettle or Dutch oven, combine boiling water,
bouillon cubes, tomatoes, garlic and onion. Stir until
bouillon cubes are dissolved. Add GARDEN VEGE-
TABLE MIX and green chili salsa. Cover and cook
over medium-high heat 15 to 20 minutes. Just before
serving, add grated cheese and stir until just melted.
Makes 6 servings.

Hearty Soup Mix

Makes a "souper" supper—great for camping!

1 (14-oz.) pkg. dry
   green split peas
1 (12-oz.) pkg.
   pearl barley
1 (14-oz.) pkg.
   alphabet macaroni
1 (12-oz.) pkg. lentils
1½ cups brown rice
4 cups dry minced
   onion

Combine ingredients in a large airtight container. Stir to evenly distribute ingredients. Label container. Store in a cool, dry place. Use within 6 months. Shake before using. Makes about 12½ cups of HEARTY SOUP MIX.

Hearty Soup Stock

6 cups water
1⅓ cups HEARTY
   SOUP MIX,
   see above
1½ tablespoons salt
2 carrots, sliced
1 or 2 stalks celery,
   chopped
1½ cups cabbage,
   shredded
2 (15-oz.) cans
   tomato sauce
1 (24-oz.) can
   vegetable juice
   cocktail
1 lb. ground beef
   or leftover meat,
   cooked, if desired

Put water in a large kettle or Dutch oven. Add HEARTY SOUP MIX and salt. Bring to a boil. Cover and simmer 1 to 1½ hours. Add carrots, celery, cabbage, tomato sauce and vegetable juice cocktail. Add cooked ground beef or other meat, if desired. Simmer 20 more minutes, until vegetables are cooked. Makes 6 to 8 servings.

MAIN DISHES

Do you hate that last-minute frenzy when you are trying to put a meal together and everyone is hungry and in a hurry? Be ready by having these skip-a-step mixes on hand to trim your preparation time to minutes.

The secret to using Make-A-Mix Cookery in your main dishes is to plan ahead. It's easy to prepare several mixes when you have the time then cook them when you're in a hurry.

Main dishes are easy with READY HAMBURGER MIX, MEAT SAUCE MIX and CHICKEN MIX. Thaw the frozen mixes in your refrigerator or microwave oven to keep them fresher. After you've used these mixes with some of our recipes, you'll probably want to adapt them to your own favorite recipes.

Company Chicken Roll-Ups are truly delicious. You can refrigerate or freeze them days before, then just fry and bake them at serving time. Expect lots of compliments!

For cooking Italian-style, you can use either ITALIAN COOKING SAUCE MIX or the slow-simmering ITALIAN MEAT SAUCE MIX in most recipes. Use PANCAKE MIX to make Monte Cristo Sandwiches!

Have you avoided Mexican cooking? MEXICAN MEAT MIX is perfect for many South-of-the-Border recipes. Our preference by far is Chimichangas, the deep-fried goodies everyone should experience!

Under More Desserts, page 209, you'll find another great idea—Turnover Fried Pies with main dish variations! Or grow your own meal with GARDEN VEGE-

TABLE MIX. To accompany your main dishes, check out the rice dishes on pages 48 to 51.

Are you a microwave cook? With microwave ovens you can cook some recipes in one-fourth the amount of time specified in the recipe. Check the manufacturer's instructions to be sure.

Spaghetti & Meatballs

Don't forget the tossed salad and garlic bread!

2 qts. water
1 teaspoon salt
1 (12-oz.) pkg. spaghetti
2 pints ITALIAN
  COOKING SAUCE
  MIX, pages 25–26
  thawed

1 container MEATBALL
  MIX, page 24, thawed
  (about 30 meatballs)
Grated Parmesan cheese,
  for garnish

Bring water to a boil in a large saucepan. Add salt and spaghetti. Cook according to package directions. In a medium saucepan, cook ITALIAN COOKING SAUCE MIX over low heat about 15 minutes. Stir in MEAT-BALL MIX and simmer 15 minutes. Put cooked spaghetti on a serving platter and pour meatballs and sauce over top. Sprinkle with grated Parmesan cheese. Makes 6 to 8 servings.

Variations

Substitute 2 (15-oz.) jars spaghetti sauce for ITAL-IAN COOKING SAUCE MIX.

Substitute 2 pints thawed ITALIAN MEAT SAUCE MIX, pages 26–27, for ITALIAN COOKING SAUCE MIX and MEATBALL MIX.

For a meatball sandwich, decrease sauce to 1 pint, omit spaghetti and serve on Italian bread.

Stuffed Manicotti Shells

For special company or your special family.

12 manicotti shells,
  cooked
Water
Salt
1 pint ricotta cheese
1 egg, beaten
¼ cup Parmesan cheese

1 tablespoon parsley
  flakes
4 cups ITALIAN
  MEAT SAUCE MIX,
  pages, 26–27, thawed
Romano and Parmesan
  cheese, for garnish

Cook manicotti shells in boiling salted water according to package directions. In a medium bowl, combine ricotta cheese, eggs, Parmesan cheese and parsley flakes. Blend well. Stuff into cooked manicotti shells. Preheat oven to 350°F (175°C). Place 1 cup of the ITALIAN MEAT SAUCE MIX in bottom of a 13″ × 9″ baking dish. Place stuffed manicotti shells on top of sauce. Pour remaining sauce over top of shells. Sprinkle with Romano and Parmesan cheese, for garnish. Cover with foil and bake 30 minutes, until heated through. Makes 6 servings.

Variation
Substitute 4 cups ITALIAN COOKING SAUCE MIX, pages 25–26, for ITALIAN MEAT SAUCE MIX.

Veal Parmigiana

Your friends will love it.

6 thin veal cutlets	Butter or olive oil
1 egg, slightly beaten	for frying
2 to 3 tablespoons milk	2 cups ITALIAN
¾ cup seasoned dry	COOKING SAUCE
breadcrumbs	MIX, pages 25–26
¾ cup grated Parmesan	8 oz. mozzarella cheese,
cheese	sliced

Pound veal cutlets until thin. Combine egg and milk in a small bowl. In another small bowl, combine dry breadcrumbs and grated Parmesan cheese. Dip veal into egg mixture, then into breadcrumbs mixture. Let veal stand at least 15 minutes before cooking. Heat butter or olive oil in a large skillet. Sauté veal cutlets in butter or oil about 2 minutes on each side until crisp. Preheat oven to 400°F (205°C). Put veal into a 13″ × 9″ baking pan. Pour ITALIAN COOKING SAUCE MIX over top. Place a slice of mozzarella cheese on each cutlet. Bake 10 to 15 minutes, until veal is golden brown and cheese is melted. Makes 4 to 6 servings.

Variation

Use veal cutlets that are already breaded and omit egg, milk, breadcrumbs and grated Parmesan cheese.

Speedy Pizza

Teenagers eat these by the dozens.

1 pint MEAT SAUCE
  MIX, page 22
6 English muffins, split
Oregano, for garnish
1 cup grated mozzarella
  cheese

Pepperoni, mushrooms,
  green peppers and
  olives, as desired

In a small saucepan, simmer MEAT SAUCE MIX about 5 minutes, until heated through. Toast English muffin halves. Spoon meat mixture generously over English muffins. Sprinkle with oregano and top with grated mozzarella cheese. Add toppings as desired. Broil about 3 to 5 minutes, until cheese is bubbly. Makes 12 individual pizzas.

Rancher's Sloppy Joes

Feed a hungry crowd!

1 pint MEAT SAUCE
  MIX, page 22, thawed
¼ cup brown sugar,
  firmly packed

2 tablespoons vinegar
½ cup ketchup
1 tablespoon mustard
6 hamburger buns

In a medium saucepan, combine MEAT SAUCE MIX, brown sugar, vinegar, ketchup and mustard. Cover and cook over medium heat about 10 minutes, until heated through. Serve over hamburger buns. Makes 6 servings.

Beef Bourguignonne

This mock bourguignonne will
appeal to the gourmets you serve.

2 tablespoons butter
  or margarine
1 cup thinly sliced onions
1 cup carrots, cut in
  thin strips
1 clove garlic, minced
1 teaspoon salt
⅛ teaspoon pepper
⅛ teaspoon marjoram
⅛ teaspoon thyme

1 cup beef broth
  or bouillon
1 (6-oz.) can mushroom
  crowns
1 pint BRAISED BEEF
  CUBE MIX, page 20
  thawed
Buttered noodles,
  sprinkled with
  poppy seeds

Melt butter or margarine in a large skillet. Sauté onions, carrots and garlic until onions are lightly browned. Add salt, pepper, marjoram, thyme, beef broth or bouillon, mushrooms and BRAISED BEEF CUBE MIX. Stir until well-blended. Cover and cook over medium heat, stirring occasionally, until vegetables are tender. Serve over hot buttered noodles sprinkled with poppy seeds. Makes 6 servings.

Monte Cristo Sandwiches

Add some pizzazz to ham and cheese sandwiches.

12 slices white bread
Mayonnaise
12 thin slices natural
  Swiss cheese
6 thin slices baked ham
6 thin slices roast turkey
2 eggs, beaten

1 cup milk
1 cup PANCAKE MIX,
  page 19
Butter for griddle
Powdered sugar,
  for garnish
Currant jelly, for garnish

Preheat griddle to 350°F (175°C). Spread 1 side of each slice of bread with a thin coating of mayonnaise. Assemble each sandwich using 2 slices of Swiss cheese, 1 slice of ham and 1 slice of turkey. Trim crusts with a sharp knife, making the edges even. Cut each sandwich in half. Set aside. Combine eggs and milk in a shallow dish. Add PANCAKE MIX. Butter griddle. Dip each sandwich into the batter. Grill about 3 to 4 minutes, until lightly browned on both sides and cheese begins to melt. Lightly sprinkle with powdered sugar and currant jelly. Makes 6 sandwiches.

Variation

Omit turkey slices and use 12 slices of ham.

How to Make Monte Cristo Sandwiches

1/Assemble sandwiches with 2 slices of Swiss cheese, 1 slice of ham and 1 slice of turkey. Trim the crusts, making the edges even.

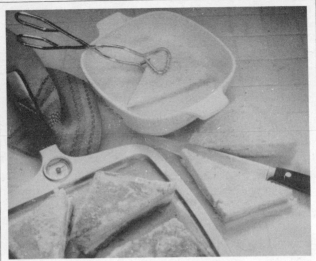

2/Dip each sandwich into the batter,
then grill until lightly browned on both sides.

3/Serve Monte Cristo Sandwiches sprinkled
with powdered sugar and topped with currant jelly.

Chicken Cacciatore

Viva la Italian!

Vegetable oil for frying
½ cup all-purpose flour
1 teaspoon salt
¼ teaspoon pepper
1 (4-lb.) fryer chicken,
  cut up

4 cups ITALIAN
COOKING SAUCE
MIX, pages 25–26,
thawed

Heat oil in a large skillet. Combine flour, salt and pepper in a plastic bag. Add chicken pieces 2 at a time and shake to coat with mixture. Brown chicken in hot oil until golden brown. Preheat oven to 350°F (175°C). Put chicken in a 13″ × 9″ baking dish. Pour ITALIAN COOKING SAUCE MIX over chicken. Cover with foil. Bake about 1 hour, until chicken is tender. Makes 4 to 6 servings.

Company Chicken Roll-Ups

Your guests will rave about these tender chicken nuggets.

½ cup WHITE SAUCE
  MIX, page 30
1 cup cool water
1 cup grated Cheddar
  cheese
1 (4-oz.) can sliced
  mushrooms, drained
6 whole chicken breasts,
  skinned and boned

Flour
1 teaspoon salt
1 egg, slightly beaten
1 cup milk
2 cups dry breadcrumbs
Vegetable oil for frying

In a small saucepan, combine WHITE SAUCE MIX with cool water. Cook over low heat until thick and smooth, stirring constantly. Add grated Cheddar cheese and mushrooms. Stir until cheese is melted. Pour into an 8-inch square pan. Chill until set. Lay large pieces of chicken breasts on a generously floured surface with sides just touching. Fill in any gaps with small pieces of chicken. Sprinkle generously with flour. Cover with plastic wrap and pound together with a wooden mallet. Roll lightly with a rolling pin to form a rectangular shape, about 8" × 20". Remove plastic wrap. Sprinkle with salt. Cut cheese mixture in ½- to ¾-inch strips. Lay about half of cheese strips along the long edge of chicken. Carefully wrap chicken around cheese mixture and roll up lengthwise like a jelly roll. With a sharp knife, cut into 2- to 3-inch pieces. Combine egg and milk in a shallow dish. Dip chicken pieces in egg mixture, then in breadcrumbs. Place on a wire rack to dry out, about 15 minutes. Preheat oven to 350°F (175°C). Fry chicken in hot oil about 1 minute on each side, until golden. Place in a 13" × 9" baking pan. Cover and bake 45 minutes, until chicken is tender. Melt remaining cheese mixture and serve over chicken rolls. Makes 8 to 10 servings.

Note:

After chicken has been breaded, it can be loosely covered and refrigerated for a day, then cooked the next day. Breaded chicken rolls can also be frozen on a baking sheet, then stored in an airtight bag in freezer. Thaw several hours, then fry and bake as directed.

Chicken Oahu

The sauce is the star of this blend of flavors from the Islands.

4 cups HERBED STUFFING MIX, page 28
1 (8-oz.) can crushed pineapple, undrained
¼ cup water
½ cup flour

½ teaspoon salt
½ teaspoon paprika
Dash of pepper
1 (2½- to 3-lb.) fryer chicken, cut up
Creamy Sauce, see below

Creamy Sauce:

1½ cups chopped celery
½ cup chopped onion
2 tablespoons chopped green pepper
½ cup water

1 (10¾-oz.) can cream of mushroom soup
½ cup sour cream
1 tablespoon soy sauce

Preheat oven to 375°F (190°C). Lightly grease a 13″ × 9″ baking dish. In a medium bowl, combine HERBED STUFFING MIX, pineapple and water. Put into prepared baking dish. In a plastic bag, combine flour, salt, paprika and dash of pepper. Add chicken pieces 2 at a time and shake to coat. Place chicken on top of stuffing mixture. Cover with foil. Bake 30 minutes. Remove foil and bake 30 more minutes. Prepare Creamy Sauce and spoon over top of chicken. Makes 6 servings.

Creamy Sauce:

In a medium skillet, combine celery, onion, green pepper and water. Cover and simmer 10 minutes. Drain off water. Add soup, sour cream and soy sauce. Heat through.

Chicken Burgers

Perfect for a Saturday afternoon lunch.

2 cups CHICKEN MIX,   1 cup barbecue sauce
  page 27, thawed   8 hamburger buns

Combine CHICKEN MIX and barbecue sauce in a medium saucepan. Cook over medium heat about 10 minutes, until heated through. Serve over hamburger buns. Makes 8 burgers.

Hawaiian Haystack

When it's time for a Polynesian buffet, put the ingredients in order and let your guests stack 'em up!

2 (10¾-oz.) cans cream   ½ cup chopped green
  of chicken soup   pepper
1 cup Chicken Broth,   ½ cup chopped green
  page 27, thawed   onion
2 cups CHICKEN MIX,   1 (20-oz.) can pineapple
  page 27, thawed   chunks, drained
4 cups cooked long-grain 1 cup grated Cheddar
  rice   cheese
1 (9½-oz.) can   ½ cup slivered almonds
  chow mein noodles   ½ cup coconut
3 medium tomatoes,   1 (2-oz.) jar pimiento,
  sliced   drained and diced,
1 cup chopped celery   if desired

Combine soup and Chicken Broth in a medium saucepan to make gravy. Stir to blend. Add CHICKEN MIX. Simmer about 8 to 10 minutes, until heated through. On 8 individual serving plates layer all ingredients. First stack rice, chow mein noodles, and chicken and gravy. Add tomatoes, celery, green pepper and green onion. Top this with pineapple chunks, grated Cheddar cheese, and more chicken and gravy, if desired. Stack almonds, coconut and pimiento on top. Makes 8 servings.

Sweet & Sour Chicken

It's time for a Hawaiian delight!

½ cup water
5 tablespoons cornstarch
¾ cup brown sugar, firmly packed
1 teaspoon salt
1 (20-oz.) can pineapple chunks, drained, reserving juice
2 cups CHICKEN MIX, page 27, thawed
2 tablespoons soy sauce
¼ cup white vinegar
2 cups Chicken Broth, page 27, thawed
2 cups water
2 cups uncooked long-grain rice
½ cup thinly sliced onion
¾ cup thinly sliced green peppers
2 large tomatoes, cut in wedges

In a small bowl, combine ½ cup water, cornstarch, brown sugar and salt. Stir until mixture is smooth. Combine with reserved pineapple juice and brown sugar mixture in a large saucepan. Cook over medium heat about 5 to 7 minutes, until mixture starts to thicken. Add CHICKEN MIX, soy sauce and vinegar. Cover and simmer 15 minutes, stirring occasionally. Put Chicken Broth and 2 cups water in a large saucepan. Add rice. Cover and cook about 25 minutes. Add pineapple chunks, onion slices and green peppers to CHICKEN MIX mixture. Cook until vegetables are slightly tender. Just before serving, stir in tomato wedges. Serve over the hot, cooked rice. Makes 8 to 10 servings.

For "just right" pasta, cook 8 ounces of pasta in 6 cups of rapidly boiling water with 4 teaspoons salt. Stir constantly for 2 minutes. Cover the pan, remove from heat and let stand 10 minutes.
Drain and rinse immediately.

Tempura

*Let this tempting Tempura lend an
Oriental flair to your dinner.*

Vegetable oil for frying
2 tablespoons shredded
  radishes and 2 table-
  spoons shredded
  turnips, or 2 table-
  spoons grated fresh
  ginger root
Oriental Sauce, see below
3 cups QUICK MIX,
  page 15
1¾ cups ice water
2 eggs, slightly beaten
½ lb. fresh shrimp,
  shelled and deveined,
  or 1 (8-oz.) pkg.
  frozen shrimp,
  thawed
¼ lb. fresh mushrooms,
  cut in half

2 carrots, peeled, cut
  lengthwise in ¼-in.
  thick sticks
1 green pepper, cut in
  ¼-in. thick strips
1 cup peeled eggplant
  strips, ¼-in. thick
½ lb. fresh asparagus
  spears, cut
1 yam or sweet potato,
  peeled, sliced in ¼-in.
  thick rounds
½ lb. fresh spinach,
  broken
½ lb. fresh green beans,
  cut

Oriental Sauce:

¼ cup soy sauce
¼ cup rice vinegar

1 tablespoon green onion,
  finely chopped

Heat 1 inch of oil to 350°F (175°C) in an electric
skillet. Put radishes and turnips or grated fresh ginger
root in a small bowl. Prepare Oriental Sauce. In a
medium bowl, combine QUICK MIX, ice water and
eggs. Beat until smooth. Pat shrimp and vegetables dry
with paper towels. Dip into batter. Fry several pieces
at a time in hot oil about 1 to 2 mintes on each side,
until golden brown. Drain on paper towels. Dip into
Oriental Sauce and then into radish-turnip mixture of
fresh ginger root. Makes about 6 servings.

Oriental Sauce:
Combine all ingredients in a small bowl. Blend well.

Sweet & Sour Meatballs

Not just plain meatballs!

1 tablespoon vegetable
  oil
1 (20-oz.) can pineapple
  chunks, drained,
  reserving juice
3 tablespoons cornstarch
1 tablespoon soy sauce
3 tablespoons vinegar

6 tablespoons water
½ cup brown sugar
1 container MEATBALL
  MIX, page 24, thawed
1 large green pepper,
  sliced
About 4 cups cooked rice

In a large skillet, combine oil and 1 cup drained pineapple juice, adding water if necessary to make 1 cup.
In a small bowl, combine cornstarch, soy sauce, vinegar, water and brown sugar. Stir into juice mixture
and cook over medium heat about 5 to 7 minutes until
thick, stirring constantly. Add MEATBALL MIX,
pineapple chunks and green pepper. Simmer 20 minutes
until heated through. Serve over hot, cooked rice.
Makes 6 servings.

Stuffed Hard Rolls

Let the kids help make these!

1 pint MEAT SAUCE
  MIX, page 22,
  thawed

1 cup grated Cheddar
  cheese
8 hard rolls, sliced

In a medium saucepan, simmer MEAT SAUCE MIX
about 10 minutes until heated through. Remove from
heat. Stir in grated Cheddar cheese. Pull a small amount
of bread from centers of hard rolls. Fill each roll with
¼ cup of meat sauce-cheese mixture. Makes 8 stuffed
rolls.

Simplified Quiche

Oo-la-la! A French delicacy made easy!

1 egg, separated
1 baked Moist Pie Crust, pages 40–41, or Flaky Pie Crust, page 39
4 strips bacon, partially cooked, chopped
1¾ cups milk or cream

1 cup grated Swiss cheese
½ teaspoon salt
¼ teaspoon paprika
1 teaspoon minced onion
Dash of cayenne pepper
3 eggs
Chicken gravy, if desired
Pimiento, for garnish

Beat egg white and brush on bottom of pie crust. Reserve egg yolk. Sprinkle bacon evenly over bottom of crust. Scald milk or cream in a medium saucepan. Reduce heat and add grated cheese. Stir until cheese is melted. Add salt, paprika, onion and cayenne pepper. Remove from heat and cool lightly. Add 3 eggs plus reserved yolk 1 at a time, beating well after each. Pour into pie crust. Bake about 45 minutes, until a toothpick inserted in center comes out clean. Serve with chicken gravy, if desired. Garnish with pimiento. Makes 1 quiche.

Self-Crust Cheese Tart

Easiest pie for a light supper.

Paprika
1 cup grated Swiss cheese
4 strips bacon, cooked and crumbled
3 eggs
¼ teaspoon salt
¼ teaspoon nutmeg, if desired

1½ cups milk
1 teaspoon instant minced onion
⅓ cup QUICK MIX, page 15

Preheat oven to 325°F (165°C). Generously butter a 9-inch pie plate. Sprinkle bottom and sides of prepared pie plate lightly with paprika. Layer Swiss cheese and bacon on bottom of pie plate. Combine eggs, salt, nutmeg, milk, onion and QUICK MIX in a blender. Blend at medium speed about 1 minute, until thoroughly mixed. Pour over cheese and bacon in pie plate. Bake 30 to 40 minutes, until a toothpick inserted in center comes out clean. Serve hot. Makes 6 servings.

Green Chili Burros

That's Mexican!

3 cups MEXICAN
MEAT MIX, pages
24–25, thawed

6 large flour tortillas

Heat MEXICAN MEAT MIX in a small saucepan. Warm tortillas 1 at a time over low heat in a very large skillet until soft and pliable. Spread ½ cup MEXICAN MEAT MIX over the lower third of each tortilla. Fold the bottom edge of each tortilla up over filling. Fold both sides toward the center and roll into a cylinder. Place on a heated plate, seam-side down. Garnish with shredded lettuce. Serve warm. Makes 6 burros.

Variation

Enchilada-style Burros: Cover burros with enchilada sauce and sprinkle with grated Cheddar cheese. Just before serving, place under broiler to melt cheese. Garnish with shredded lettuce and sour cream.

Chalupa

Top this with "hot" sauce for a really spicy meal.

1 lb. dry pinto beans
3 cups MEXICAN
MEAT MIX, pages
24–25, thawed
1 teaspoon salt
1 tablespoon chili powder
1 (10-oz.) bag corn chips

1 cup grated longhorn or
Monterey Jack cheese
½ cup chopped onion
Shredded lettuce
2 tomatoes, chopped

Wash beans, put in a large pan and cover with water. Soak overnight. Cover and cook over low heat about 4 to 5 hours until beans are tender. Add water if needed. Add MEXICAN MEAT MIX, salt and chili powder. Cook uncovered about 1 hour, stirring occasionally, until heated through. Serve in small bowls over crisp corn chips. Garnish with cheese, onion, lettuce and tomatoes. Makes 8 servings.

Variation

Substitute 3 (15-oz.) cans pinto beans for dry pinto beans. Omit soaking and cooking until tender.

Chimichangas

These won the Southwest!

6 large flour tortillas
3 cups MEXICAN MEAT MIX, pages 24–25, thawed
Vegetable oil for frying
Shredded lettuce
1 (7-oz.) can green chili salsa

2 tomatoes, chopped
1 cup Guacamole, see below
½ pint sour cream
6 ripe olives, for garnish

Guacamole:

2 ripe avocados, pared and mashed
1 teaspoon lemon juice

Salt and pepper to taste
Few drops of Tabasco® sauce

Warm tortillas in oven about 5 minutes. Heat MEXICAN MEAT MIX in a small saucepan. Heat ½-inch deep oil to 400°F (205°C) in a large skillet. Spread about ½ cup MEXICAN MEAT MIX over the lower third of each tortilla. Fold the bottom edges of each tortilla up over filling. Fold both sides toward the center and roll into a cylinder. Secure rolled tortillas with a toothpick. Fry 2 chimichangas at a time in hot oil about 2 minutes until golden and crisp. Drain on paper towels. Serve hot over a layer of shredded lettuce. Top with green chili salsa, tomatoes, Guacamole and sour cream. Garnish each with an olive. Makes 6 chimichangas.

Guacamole:

Combine all ingredients in a small bowl.

How to Make Chimichangas

1/Fold the bottom edge of each tortilla over the meat filling, and fold both sides toward the center.

2/Roll each tortilla into a cylinder. Secure with a toothpick. Serve Chimichangas over letturce, topped with green chili salsa, tomatoes, Guacamole and sour cream.

Sour Cream Enchiladas

MEXICAN MEAT MIX wins again!

1 (10-oz.) can enchilada
    sauce
1 (16-oz.) can whole
    tomatoes, undrained
    and finely chopped
Vegetable oil for frying
12 corn tortillas

3 cups MEXICAN
    MEAT MIX, pages
    24–25, thawed
1½ cups grated Cheddar
    cheese
1½ cups sour cream

Combine enchilada sauce and chopped tomatoes in a medium saucepan. Cook over medium heat until mixture boils. Reduce heat and simmer. Heat oil over medium-high heat in a small skillet. Dip one tortilla at a time in hot oil for several seconds, then dip in hot enchilada sauce mixture. Set aside. Heat MEXICAN MEAT MIX in a small saucepan. Place about ¼ cup MEXICAN MEAT MIX on each tortilla and sprinkle with 2 tablespoons grated Cheddar cheese. Roll up and place close together in a shallow casserole dish, seam-side down. Pour remaining sauce over enchiladas. Sprinkle with additional grated cheese. Bake about 15 minutes, until bubbly. Spoon sour cream over enchiladas and serve hot. Makes about 6 servings.

Tacos Supreme

For a super Mexican sandwich!

Vegetable oil for frying
3 cups MEXICAN
    MEAT MIX, pages
    24–25, thawed
12 to 15 corn tortillas
2 cups grated Cheddar
    cheese

Shredded lettuce
2 fresh tomatoes,
    chopped
¼ cup chopped green
    onion
1 (7-oz.) can green chili
    salsa

Heat 2 inches of oil to 375°F (190°C) in a large skillet. Heat MEXICAN MEAT MIX in a medium saucepan. Fry tortillas in hot oil. Using tongs, fold tortillas in half, then immediately open to 45-degree angle. Fry about 1 minute, until crisp. Drain on paper towels. Place 2 tablespoons MEXICAN MEAT MIX in each cooked tortilla. Top with grated cheese, lettuce, tomatoes, green onion and green chili salsa. Makes 12 to 15 tacos.

Variation

For added convenience, use prefried, formed corn tortillas instead of forming your own.

Taco Salad

Perfect for a hot summer night.

2 cups READY HAM-
  BURGER MIX,
  page 17, thawed
1 (7-oz.) can green chili
  salsa
1 head of lettuce, torn
  into bite-size pieces
3 large tomatoes, chopped
1 large avocado, chopped
4 to 5 green onions,
  chopped

2 cups grated Cheddar
  cheese
1 (15-oz.) can kidney
  beans, drained
1 (10-oz.) pkg. tortilla
  chips
Salad Dressing of your
  choice

Combine READY HAMBURGER MIX and green chili salsa in a medium skillet. In a large salad bowl, combine lettuce, tomatoes, avocado, green onions, grated cheese and kidney beans. Add hamburger mixture. Toss gently. Add tortilla chips and top with salad dressing of your choice. Makes 8 servings.

Spoon Tacos

A great dish for camping.

2 cups READY HAM-
  BURGER MIX,
  page 17, thawed
1 (10-oz.) pkg. tortilla
  chips or corn chips
1 small head of lettuce,
  shredded

1 large tomato, diced
1 cup grated Cheddar
  cheese
1 (7-oz.) can green chili
  salsa

Heat READY HAMBURGER MIX in a medium skillet. On individual plates, layer READY HAMBUR-
GER MIX, tortilla chips or corn chips, lettuce, tomato
pieces and cheese. Top with green chili salsa to taste.
Makes 6 servings.

Stuffed Green Peppers

This colorful dish will satisfy your appetite.

1 pint MEAT SAUCE
  MIX, page 22, thawed
2 cups cooked rice, or
  1 can whole kernel
  corn, drained
6 to 8 cups water

8 green peppers, seeds
  and membranes
  removed
½ cup grated Cheddar
  cheese

Preheat oven to 350°F (175°C). In a small saucepan,
simmer MEAT SAUCE MIX and cooked rice about
10 minutes, until heated through. Bring water to a
rapid boil in a large saucepan. Put green peppers into
water a few at a time and boil about 10 minutes. Drain.
Fill green peppers with warmed MEAT SAUCE MIX
and rice. Top with grated cheese. Bake in a shallow
pan 10 to 15 minutes. Makes 8 stuffed green peppers.

Garden Supper

An excellent meal for a fall evening.

¼ cup butter or
   margarine
1 medium onion, chopped
¼ cup all-purpose flour
1½ cups milk

½ teaspoon salt
3 cups GARDEN VEGE-
   TABLE MIX, page 29,
   thawed and drained
Cooked rice

Melt butter or margarine in a medium saucepan. Sauté onion until clear. Add flour and stir to blend well. Add milk. Cook about 3 minutes, stirring constantly, until thick and smooth. Add salt and GARDEN VEGE-TABLE MIX. Cook uncovered about 5 minutes, stirring occasionally, until vegetables are crisp-tender. Serve over hot cooked rice. Makes 4 to 5 servings.

Supper Stuffing

Stuff your favorite poultry
or use as a side dish to any meal.

1 teaspoon instant chicken
   bouillon
¾ cup boiling water
6 tablespoons butter
   or margarine
4 large stalks celery,
   finely chopped

7 cups HERBED
   STUFFING MIX,
   page 28
Turkey or roasting
   chicken, if desired

Dissolve bouillon in boiling water. Melt butter or margarine in a medium skillet. Sauté celery until crisp-tender. In a large bowl, combine HERBED STUFF-ING MIX, bouillon-water mixture and celery. Toss lightly. Use for stuffing turkey or chicken, if desired. Or preheat oven to 350°F (175°C) and put mixture in a lightly buttered casserole. Bake 30 minutes, until heated through.

CASSEROLES

Traditionally, a casserole has been synonymous with convenience and economy. There are endless ways to put together a multitude of ingredients to form a casserole. We totally approve of combining ingredients in such a manner to create a meal—but not in any hodge-podge way!

With mixes, casseroles can be gourmet fare. Choose some recipes from this section that appeal to you, make the Master Mixes and store them until it's time to use them. When planning and preparing meals, you'll be amazed at the time your already-prepared mixes have saved you. We suggest making CHICKEN MIX and MEAT SAUCE MIX soon. Make 5 or 6 casseroles from each!

You'll taste the unique texture combination of chow mein noodles, cashew nuts and tender, moist chicken in Chicken-Cashew Casserole. The Layered Casserole Complete is as delicious as it looks. All this convenience with no sacrifice in taste!

Don't be overwhelmed if you need to prepare for a crowd. With mixes, you just thaw additional containers of the same mix to serve as many people as you like. They'll wonder how you can entertain with such ease.

Western Beef Stew

A thick, beefy stew that tastes like it simmered all day.

5 medium potatoes, pared and diced	¼ cup butter or margarine, melted
6 medium carrots, pared and sliced	1 cup fresh sliced mushrooms, or 1 (4-oz.) can mushrooms
Water	
1 small onion, thinly sliced	2 pints BRAISED BEEF CUBE MIX, page 20, thawed
½ cup chopped celery	

Combine potatoes and carrots in a large saucepan. Add just enough water to cover vegetables. Cook about 12 to 15 minutes, until tender. In a small saucepan, sauté onion and celery in melted butter or margarine, until slightly tender. Add mushrooms and sauté 2 more minutes. Drain liquid from potatoes and carrots. Add sautéed vegetables to potatoes and carrots. Stir in BRAISED BEEF CUBE MIX. Simmer about 15 minutes, until heated through. Serve hot. Makes 6 to 8 servings.

Variation

Beef Stew Pie: Put ingredients in a 13″ × 9″ baking pan. Top with Moist Pie Crust, page 40, or Flaky Pie Crust, page 39. Flute edges. Cut slits in crust. Bake at 400°F (205°C) 30 to 45 minutes, until crust is golden brown.

Meatball Stew

Time for some good home cooking.

¼ cup water	2 cups pared and sliced carrots
2 tablespoons flour	
1 beef bouillon cube	2 onions, quartered
1 (1-lb.) can tomatoes	1 cup sliced celery
1 container MEATBALL MIX, page 24, thawed, (about 30 meatballs)	1 cup peeled and cubed potatoes

In a medium saucepan, combine water, flour and bouillon. Stir until well-blended. Add tomatoes and cook about 5 minutes, until mixture thickens and boils, stirring constantly. Add MEATBALL MIX, carrots, onions, celery and potatoes. Cover and simmer 15 minutes. Preheat oven to 350°F (175°C). Pour into a 3-quart casserole. Cover and bake 1½ hours. Makes 6 to 8 servings.

Layered Casserole Complete

A hearty dinner for any family.

1 pint MEAT SAUCE MIX, page 22, thawed	2 cups mashed potatoes
1 (16-oz.) can French-cut green beans, drained, or 1 (10-oz.) pkg. frozen green beans	1 cup grated Cheddar cheese

Preheat oven to 350°F (175°C). Lightly butter a 1½-quart casserole. Layer casserole with MEAT SAUCE MIX, green beans and mashed potatoes. Sprinkle grated cheese on top. Bake 25 to 30 minutes, until bubbly. Makes 4 servings.

Hamburger Trio Skillet

Quick, easy and good.

1 pint MEAT SAUCE MIX, page 22, thawed	¼ teaspoon thyme
2 cups cooked rice	½ cup chopped green pepper
1 (17-oz.) can whole kernel corn	

Combine all ingredients in a medium skillet. Cover and cook over medium heat about 10 to 15 minutes, until heated through. Serve from skillet. Makes 4 to 6 servings.

Hamburger-Noodle Skillet

Excellent for a busy day.

1 pint MEAT SAUCE
  MIX, page 22, thawed
2 cups cooked noodles
2 cups cooked mixed
  vegetables, with liquid
1 (8-oz.) can seasoned
  tomato sauce

½ cup grated Cheddar
  cheese
1 teaspoon chopped
  parsley

In a medium skillet, combine MEAT SAUCE MIX, cooked noodles, cooked mixed vegetables and tomato sauce. Cover and cook over medium heat about 10 to 15 minutes, stirring occasionally, until heated through. Sprinkle grated cheese and parsley on top. Do not stir. Cover and heat just long enough to melt cheese. Serve from skillet. Makes 4 to 6 servings.

Saturday Stroganoff

Stroganoff lovers will love the convenience of this dish.

2 cups READY HAM-
  BURGER MIX,
  page 21, thawed
1 (10¾ oz.) can cream
  of celery soup
1 (10¾ oz.) can cream
  of mushroom soup

¾ cup milk
1 pint sour cream
Cooked noodles
Poppy seeds, for garnish

In a large saucepan, combine READY HAMBURGER MIX, cream of celery soup, cream of mushroom soup and milk. Stir until well-blended. Simmer about 10 minutes. Just before serving, add sour cream. Simmer 2 minutes. Serve over cooked noodles garnished with poppy seeds. Makes 4 to 6 servings.

Braised Beef Stroganoff

This becomes a favorite after just one bite.

2 tablespoons butter
  or margarine
1 medium onion,
  finely chopped
½ lb. sliced mushrooms

1 pint **BRAISED BEEF**
  CUBE MIX, page 20,
  thawed
1 cup sour cream
Cooked, buttered noodles

In a large skillet, melt butter or margarine over medium heat. Add onion and mushrooms. Sauté until onion is lightly browned. Stir in BRAISED BEEF CUBE MIX. Simmer 15 minutes. Just before serving, stir in sour cream. Serve over hot, buttered noodles. Makes 6 servings.

Last-Minute Lasagne

The blend of flavors is superb.

6 cups **ITALIAN MEAT**
  SAUCE MIX, pages
  26–27, thawed
1 (8-oz.) pkg. lasagne
  noodles, cooked

1 lb. ricotta cheese
¾ lb. grated mozzarella
  cheese
1 cup grated **Romano**
  and Parmesan cheese

Preheat oven to 350°F (175°C). Lightly butter a 13" × 9" baking pan. Spread one-third of ITALIAN MEAT SAUCE MIX in bottom of pan. Cover with one-third of lasagne noodles. Add one-third of ricotta cheese, thinned with water for easier spreading if necessary. Add one-third of mozzarella cheese and one-third of Romano and Parmesan cheese. Repeat layers twice, topping with Romano and Parmesan cheese. Cover with foil. Bake 30 to 35 minutes, until heated through. Let stand 10 minutes before serving. Makes 8 to 10 servings.

Variation

Substitute 6 cups ITALIAN COOKING SAUCE MIX for ITALIAN MEAT SAUCE MIX.

Enchilada Casserole

A simple introduction to Mexican cookery.

1 (6-oz.) pkg. corn chips (¾ cup)

2 cups READY HAMBURGER MIX, page 21, thawed

1 (15-oz.) can chili with beans

1 (10-oz.) can enchilada sauce

1 (8-oz.) can tomato sauce

1 cup sour cream

½ cup grated Cheddar cheese

Preheat oven to 375°F (190°C). Lightly butter a 2-quart casserole. Crush ½ cup of the corn chips and reserve for top. In a medium bowl, combine remaining corn chips, READY HAMBURGER MIX, chili, enchilada sauce and tomato sauce. Pour into prepared casserole. Bake about 20 minutes, until heated through. Remove from heat. Spread sour cream on top. Sprinkle with grated cheese and reserved crushed corn chips. Bake 5 more minutes until cheese is melted. Makes 6 servings.

To save time when preparing casseroles, grate a large amount of cheese at one time. Freeze it in individual bags in the freezer.

Tamale Pie

*Your family will be delighted with
this unique blend of cornbread and meat sauce.*

1 pint MEAT SAUCE
   MIX, page 22, thawed
1 cup cream-style corn or
   1 cup whole kernel
   corn, drained
1 medium green pepper,
   chopped

1 teaspoon chili powder
1½ cups canned tomatoes
1 cup chopped ripe olives
½ cup grated
   Cheddar cheese
Cornbread Topping,
   see below

Cornbread Topping:
2½ cups CORNMEAL
   MIX, pages 17–18

1 egg
1¼ cups milk

Preheat oven to 375°F (190°C). Lightly butter a 2-quart casserole. In a medium bowl, combine MEAT SAUCE MIX, corn, green pepper, chili powder, canned tomatoes and olives. Stir well. Put into prepared casserole. Top with grated cheese. Prepare Cornbread Topping and spoon over meat mixture. Bake 35 to 45 minutes, until golden brown. Makes 6 to 8 servings.

Cornbread Topping:

Put CORNMEAL MIX in a medium bowl. Combine egg and milk in a small bowl. Add to CORNMEAL MIX. Stir until just blended; batter should be lumpy.

Chili Con Carne

Warms you from the inside out.

1 pint MEAT SAUCE
   MIX, page 22, thawed
2 (15½-oz.) cans red
   kidney beans

1½ teaspoons chili
   powder, more if
   desired

Combine ingredients in a medium saucepan. Cover and cook over medium heat about 15 minutes, until heated through. Makes 6 servings.

How to Make Tamale Pie

1/Before you combine the ingredients, chop the green pepper and olives, and shred or grate the Cheddar cheese.

2/Combine the ingredients in a medium bowl,
then spoon into a buttered casserole dish.

3/Sprinkle cheese over the mixture and spoon
Cornbread Topping over the top.

Spaghetti Casserole

Spaghetti for a crowd!

1 (12-oz.) pkg. spaghetti
Water, lightly salted
1 tablespoon sugar
3 cups grated Cheddar
  cheese
1 pint READY HAM-
  BURGER MIX, page
  21, thawed

1 (2¼-oz.) can
  mushrooms
1 (10½-oz.) can tomato
  soup
½ cup milk
1 (15-oz.) jar spaghetti
  sauce

Preheat oven to 350°F (175°C). Butter a 2½- to 3-quart casserole. Cook spaghetti in lightly salted water according to package directions. Put half of cooked spaghetti in bottom of prepared casserole. Sprinkle with half the sugar. Sprinkle half the grated cheese on top, then half the READY HAMBURGER MIX, then half the mushrooms. Repeat layers. In a small bowl, combine tomato soup, milk and spaghetti sauce. Pour over entire casserole. If necessary, add more milk during baking to keep casserole moist. Bake 1 hour, until bubbly. Makes 6 to 8 servings.

Busy Day Casserole

You couldn't find an easier supper.

2 cups READY HAM-
  BURGER MIX, page
  21, thawed
1 (26¼-oz.) can
  spaghetti

1 (31-oz.) can pork and
  beans
¾ cup ketchup
2 teaspoons chili powder

Preheat oven to 350°F (175°C). Lightly butter a 2-quart casserole. In casserole, combine READY HAMBURGER MIX, spaghetti, pork and beans, ketchup and chili powder. Stir to blend. Heat about 20 minutes, until bubbly. Makes 6 servings.

Chicken Continental

CHICKEN MIX makes it easier.

1 (10¾-oz.) can cream
   of chicken soup
2 tablespoons grated
   onion
1 teaspoon salt
Dash of pepper
1 tablespoon parsley
   flakes

¼ teaspoon thyme
2 cups Chicken Broth,
   page 27, thawed
2 cups CHICKEN MIX,
   page 27, thawed
2 cups instant rice

Preheat oven to 375°F (190°C). Lightly butter a 2-quart casserole. In a medium bowl, combine cream of chicken soup, onion, salt, pepper, parsley flakes, thyme and Chicken Broth. Stir until well-blended. Add CHICKEN MIX and instant rice. Put in prepared casserole. Cover and bake about 30 minutes, until rice is tender. Makes 6 servings.

Club Chicken Casserole

Keep this recipe up front!

2 cups Chicken Broth,
   page 27, thawed
1 cup uncooked long-
   grain rice
3 tablespoons butter or
   margarine
3 tablespoons all-purpose
   flour
1½ teaspoons salt
1⅔ cups evaporated milk

2 cups CHICKEN MIX,
   page 27, thawed
1 (10-oz.) pkg. frozen
   chopped broccoli,
   cooked and drained
1 (3-oz.) can sliced
   mushrooms, drained
¼ cup toasted slivered
   almonds
Paprika, for garnish

Preheat oven to 350°F (175°C). Lightly butter an 11″ × 7″ baking pan. Combine Chicken Broth and rice in a large saucepan. Cook about 25 minutes, until rice is tender. Melt butter or margarine in a large saucepan. Gradually stir in flour and salt. Gradually add evaporated milk. Cook over medium heat about 5 minutes, stirring constantly, until mixture thickens and boils. Add CHICKEN MIX, cooked rice mixture, broccoli and mushrooms. Put in prepared baking pan. Top with toasted almonds and paprika. Bake 30 to 35 minutes, until bubbly. Makes 8 servings.

Variation

Substitute 1 (10-oz.) pkg. frozen peas for broccoli.

Chicken Strata

Give it a layered look!

1 (2½ - to 3-lb.) stewing chicken	1 teaspoon salt
1 carrot, pared and sliced	½ cup milk
1 onion, sliced	2 eggs, slightly beaten
2 teaspoons salt	3 cups HERBED STUFFING MIX, page 28
2 qts. water	
2 cups chicken broth	1 cup dry breadcrumbs
½ cup butter or margarine	¼ cup butter or margarine, melted
½ cup flour	

In a large saucepan, combine chicken, carrot, onion, 2 teaspoons salt and water. Cover and cook over high heat about 5 minutes, until water boils. Reduce heat and simmer 1½ to 2 hours, until chicken is tender. Remove from heat. Strain broth and refrigerate until fat can be skimmed from top. Cool chicken. Remove meat from bones, and discard bones and skin. Melt ½ cup butter or margarine in a medium saucepan. Stir in flour and 1 teaspoon salt. Cook 1 minute, stirring constantly. Gradually stir in broth and milk. Cook over medium heat about 3 to 5 minutes, stirring constantly, until mixture thickens. Remove from heat and gradually add half of mixture to beaten eggs in a small bowl. Mix well. Blend egg mixture slowly into the remaining hot mixture in the saucepan. Cook 3 to 4 minutes. Remove from heat. Preheat oven to 375°F (190°C). Butter a 2½-quart casserole. Put HERBED STUFFING MIX in casserole. Pour half the sauce over stuffing. Add pieces of deboned chicken. Add remaining sauce. In a small bowl, mix breadcrumbs with ¼ cup melted butter or margarine and sprinkle over casserole. Bake 20 to 30 minutes, until bubbly. Makes 8 servings.

Mexican Chicken Bake

You'll need corn tortillas for this one.

1 (10¾-oz.) can cream of mushroom soup	1 large onion, finely chopped
1 (10¾-oz.) can cream of chicken soup	1 (7-oz.) can green chili salsa
2¾ cups milk	2½ cups grated Cheddar cheese
2 cups CHICKEN MIX, page 27, thawed	12 corn tortillas, each cut into 8 pieces
½ teaspoon salt	

Preheat oven to 350°F (175°C). Lightly butter a 2-quart casserole. In a medium bowl, combine cream of mushroom soup, cream of chicken soup and milk. Stir to blend well. Add CHICKEN MIX, salt, onion, green chili salsa and 2 cups of the grated cheese. Layer tortilla pieces and chicken mixture alternately in prepared casserole, topping with chicken mixture. Top with remaining grated cheese. Bake 35 to 45 minutes, until bubbly. Makes 8 servings.

Variation

For a "hotter" flavor, substitute 1 (4-oz.) can diced green chilies for green chili salsa.

How to Make Chicken A La King

1/ Melt butter or margarine in a skillet, then add chopped celery and sliced mushrooms. Sauté until tender.

2/ Simmer the ingredients in chicken broth 10 minutes. Serve in baked puff pastry shells for a luncheon or over hot cooked rice for dinner.

Chicken A La King

A dish truly fit for a king!

½ cup butter or
   margarine
1 cup chopped celery
1 (4-oz.) can mushrooms
   or ¼ lb. fresh sliced
   mushrooms
½ cup all-purpose flour
2 cups Chicken Broth,
   page 27, thawed
2 cups CHICKEN MIX,
   page 27, thawed

1 cup milk
¼ cup chopped pimiento,
   if desired
1 tablespoon parsley
   flakes
Cooked rice
Slivered almonds, for
   garnish

Melt butter or margarine in a large skillet. Add celery and mushrooms. Sauté until tender. Blend in flour and let simmer 1 minute. Slowly add Chicken Broth. Cook about 3 to 5 minutes, stirring constantly until thick. Add CHICKEN MIX, milk, pimiento, if desired, and parsley flakes. Simmer 10 minutes. Serve over hot cooked rice. Garnish with slivered almonds. Makes 6 servings.

Variation

For a party luncheon, serve in baked puff pastry shells.

Chicken-Cashew Casserole

*A catchy combination of cashew nuts
and chow mein noodles.*

2 (10¾-oz.) cans cream
   of mushroom soup
1¼ cups Chicken Broth,
   page 27, thawed
½ cup chopped onion
2 cups chopped celery

2 cups CHICKEN MIX,
   page 27, thawed
1 (9½-oz.) can chow
   mein noodles
1 cup cashew nuts

Preheat oven to 350°F (175°C). Lightly butter a 2-quart casserole. In a medium bowl, combine cream of mushroom soup, Chicken Broth or water, onion and celery. Stir to blend. Add CHICKEN MIX, chow mein noodles and cashew nuts. Pour into prepared casserole. Bake, uncovered, 45 minutes. Makes 6 to 8 servings.

Hot Chicken Salad

It's versatile as an appetizer or luncheon or main dish.

2 cups CHICKEN MIX,
    page 27, thawed
2 cups chopped celery
1 cup sliced almonds
1 tablespoon minced
    onion
2 tablespoons lemon juice

1 teaspoon salt
1¼ cups mayonnaise
4 hard-boiled eggs,
    chopped
1 cup grated sharp
    Cheddar cheese

Preheat oven to 400°F (205°C). Lightly butter a 2-quart casserole. In a medium bowl, combine CHICKEN MIX, celery, almonds, onion, lemon juice, salt and mayonnaise. Mix well. Add chopped eggs and toss lightly. Put mixture into prepared casserole dish. Top with grated cheese. Bake, uncovered, 20 to 25 minutes. Makes 6 servings.

Variation

Hot Chicken Salad Boats: Combine all ingredients except cheese and bake as directed. Prepare Cream Puffs Supreme, pages 215–216. Spoon chicken mixture into cream puffs. Top with cheese and broil until cheese is melted. Serve warm. Makes 10 large servings or 30 appetizers.

To prevent macaroni or rice from boiling over, add a small amount of butter or margarine to the water.

Tuna-Cheese Swirls

A treat for your eyes as well as your mouth.

1 (12½-oz.) can light
  tuna, drained
1 cup frozen peas
1 (10½-oz.) can chicken-
  rice soup
1½ cups QUICK MIX,
  page 15
⅓ cup milk or water
¾ cup grated Cheddar
  cheese

Preheat oven to 425°F (220°C). Butter a 1½-quart
casserole. Combine tuna, peas and chicken-rice soup
in a medium bowl. Pour into prepared casserole. In a
small bowl, combine QUICK MIX and milk or water.
Stir until blended. On a lightly floured surface, knead
dough gently 10 times. Roll out to 6″ × 10″ rectangle, about ¼-inch thick. Sprinkle with grated cheese
and roll like a jelly roll. Seal edge. Cut into ½-inch
slices. Place slices on top of casserole. Bake 15 to 20
minutes, until biscuits are golden brown. Makes 4 to 6
servings.

Seafood Rice Puffs

A favorite for company.

Cream Puffs Supreme,
  pages 215–216
2 cups cooked rice
½ cup chopped green
  pepper
1 cup chopped celery
½ cup finely chopped
  onion
1 (4½-oz.) can water
  chestnuts, drained
  and sliced
2 (4½-oz.) cans shrimp,
  drained
1 (6½-oz.) can crab
  meat, drained
1 cup mayonnaise
1 cup tomato juice
¼ teaspoon salt
⅛ teaspoon pepper
1 tablespoon butter or
  margarine, melted
½ cup sliced almonds
1 cup grated Cheddar
  cheese
Paprika, for garnish

Prepare Cream Puffs Supreme. Preheat oven to 350°F (175°C). Butter a 2½-quart casserole. Combine rice, chopped green pepper, celery, onion, water chestnuts, shrimp, crab, mayonnaise, tomato juice, salt and pepper. Spoon into prepared casserole. Melt butter or margarine over medium heat in a small skillet. Stir in almonds until light brown. Place on top of casserole. Bake, uncovered, about 25 minutes. Keep warm. Just before serving, spoon mixture into cream puffs. Top with grated cheese and paprika. Broil until cheese is melted. Serve warm. Makes 10 large servings or 30 appetizers.

Zucchini Casserole

A perfect accompaniment to any
meat dish. Or serve it as a main dish!

4 medium zucchini, sliced ½-in. thick	2¼ cups HERBED STUFFING MIX, page 28
¾ cup pared and sliced carrots	1 (10¾-oz.) can cream of chicken soup
Water, salted	½ cup sour cream
½ cup chopped onion	
6 tablespoons butter or margarine	

In a medium saucepan, put zucchini and carrots in enough boiling, salted water to cover them. Cover pan and simmer about 15 minutes, until vegetables are tender. Drain. In a large saucepan, sauté onion in 4 tablespoons of the butter or margarine until tender. Stir in 1½ cups of the HERBED STUFFING MIX, cream of chicken soup and sour cream. Gently stir in zucchini. Preheat oven to 350°F (175°C). Lightly butter a 1½-quart casserole. Put mixture into casserole. Melt remaining butter or margarine in a small saucepan. Add remaining HERBED STUFFING MIX to butter or margarine. Toss gently and sprinkle over casserole. Bake 30 to 40 minutes. Makes 6 to 8 servings.

Scallop Casserole

A deep-sea delicacy.

1 cup chopped onion
1 tablespoon butter or
    margarine
½ cup water
½ teaspoon salt
1 lb. frozen scallops,
    thawed

4 eggs, slightly beaten
2 cups HERBED
    STUFFING MIX,
    page 28
4 slices Swiss cheese

In a medium saucepan, sauté onion in butter or margarine until tender. Add water and salt. Bring to a boil and add scallops. Cook 5 minutes over medium-high heat. Preheat oven to 350°F (175°C). Lightly butter a 2-quart casserole. Combine eggs and HERBED STUFFING MIX in casserole. Stir in scallop mixture. Bake 25 to 30 minutes. Remove from oven. Top with cheese slices. Return to oven just long enough to melt cheese. Makes 4 servings.

Spring Vegetable Bake

Just right for tonight's menu.

¼ cup butter or
    margarine
¼ cup all-purpose flour
1 teaspoon salt
Dash of pepper
1½ cups milk
⅓ cup grated Cheddar
    cheese

2 tablespoons grated
    Parmesan cheese
2 cups GARDEN VEGE-
    TABLE MIX, page 29,
    thawed and drained
2 cups dry breadcrumbs
4 tablespoons melted
    butter or margarine

Preheat oven to 350°F (175°C). Butter a 1½-quart casserole. Melt ¼ cup butter or margarine over low heat in a medium saucepan. Blend in flour, salt and pepper. Add milk all at once. Cook quickly, stirring constantly until mixture thickens. Remove from heat and stir in grated Cheddar cheese and grated Parmesan cheese. Add GARDEN VEGETABLE MIX and pour into prepared casserole. Combine breadcrumbs with 4 tablespoons melted butter or margarine. Sprinkle on top of casserole. Bake, uncovered, about 30 minutes. Makes 4 to 5 servings.

Potatoes Au Gratin

Rich in cheese sauce.

½ cup WHITE SAUCE
  MIX, page 30
1 cup cool water
1 (10½-oz.) can cream
  of chicken soup
½ cup grated Cheddar
  cheese

4 cups cooked, pared and
  cubed potatoes
1 tablespoon parsley
  flakes

Preheat oven to 350°F (175°C). Butter a 2-quart casserole. Combine WHITE SAUCE MIX and cool water in a small saucepan. Cook over low heat about 3 to 5 minutes, stirring constantly, until thick and smooth. In a medium bowl, combine white sauce, cream of chicken soup and grated cheese. Put cooked potatoes in casserole dish. Pour cheese mixture over. Stir gently to coat potatoes. Sprinkle parsley on top. Bake 20 to 30 minutes, until sides are bubbly and cheese is melted. Makes 6 servings.

COOKIES

Be a super cook by filling your home with the tempting aroma of freshly baked cookies. They speak a language that says "welcome." In this chapter you'll find chewy cookies, chocolate cookies, sugar cookies, spicy cookies, coconut cookies, cereal cookies plus shaped, rolled, drop and bar cookies!

If you're looking for a way to introduce cooking to your children, BASIC COOKIE MIX is made to order. They'll hardly have a chance to make a mess! Successes right from the beginning will motivate them to move on to more challenging mixes.

Time to build a house! We'll tell you a secret: Gingerbread Houses are easy to make! Don't tell anyone—just give them one! Populate your house with Gingerbread Boys, the highlight of holidays. These little fellows are fun to decorate.

Our brownies come with bunches of topping ideas, so you just have to try them. Date-Filled Drop Cookies are a breeze—maybe the easiest filled cookies you ever made. If oatmeal cookies are your favorites, make several kinds from OATMEAL COOKIE MIX. Or use OATMEAL MIX to make Caramelita Oatmeal Bars.

Before you sit down to indulge in a plate of cookies, make a beverage worthy of your talent to go with them. See pages 45 to 48.

Gingerbread House
(Not to Scale)

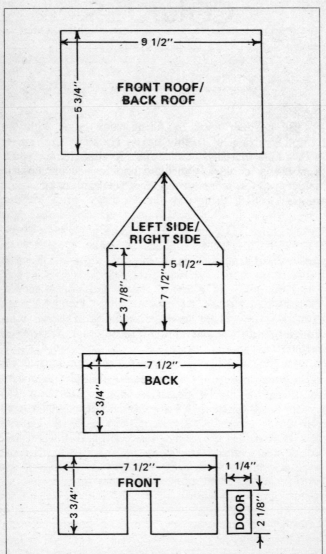

FRONT ROOF/
BACK ROOF

9 1/2"

5 3/4"

LEFT SIDE/
RIGHT SIDE

5 1/2"

3 7/8"

7 1/2"

BACK

7 1/2"

3 3/4"

FRONT

7 1/2"

3 3/4"

1 1/4"

DOOR

2 1/8"

Gingerbread House *Photo opposite.*

Here's a dream house you can build.

6 cups GINGERBREAD MIX, page 31	2 eggs, slightly beaten
⅔ cup molasses	1 cup flour
	Icing Mortar, see below

Icing Mortar:

3 egg whites, room temperature	1 lb. powdered sugar
½ teaspoon cream of tartar	

Cut house patterns from lightweight cardboard according to dimensions given below. Preheat oven to 350°F (175°C). Lightly grease baking sheets. In a medium bowl, combine GINGERBREAD MIX, molasses, eggs and flour. Blend well. Divide dough into 4 balls. Place each ball on a baking sheet. Cover with wax paper and roll out about ¼-inch thick. Dough should be smooth, without air bubbles. Bake about 7 minutes, until edges are browned. Place cardboard patterns on hot gingerbread and cut immediately. Carefully loosen pieces and put on wire racks to dry overnight. Prepare Icing Mortar. With Icing Mortar, decorate sides and roof on a flat surface. Let decorated pieces dry 3 to 4 hours. Cut a 12″ × 14″ base from heavy cardboard; cover with aluminum foil. Trace around roof pattern on center of base to indicate size and placement of house. Put a row of Icing Mortar along back, left side and front of house on base. On the back of the left wall, put a generous row of icing along both side edges; stand wall in place in Icing Mortar and prop with a glass. Repeat for back and front of house, and prop with glasses. Put door in place, slightly open. Put a row of Icing Mortar along right side of house on base. Put icing along both side edges and stand right wall in place. Make sure house is squared on floor plan. Let Icing Mortar harden about 5 to 10 minutes. Remove glasses. Attach roof 1 side at a time using Icing Mortar to hold in position. Support roof in place with a glass. Let stand 5 minutes before attaching other part of roof. Makes 1 Gingerbread House, plus extra gingerbread.

Icing Mortar:

Combine egg whites and cream of tartar in a small bowl. Beat at high speed 7 to 10 minutes until very stiff. Gradually add powdered sugar and continue beating. While decorating, keep bowl covered with a damp cloth to prevent drying.

Gingerbread Boys

*Children love to decorate these. "Paint" on
the glaze and decorate with candies and raisins.*

3 cups GINGERBREAD MIX, page 31	1 egg, slightly beaten
⅓ cup molasses	¼ cup flour
	Icing Glaze, see below

Icing Glaze:

1 cup sifted powdered sugar	2 tablespoons hot water
	½ teaspoon vanilla

Preheat oven to 350°F (175°C). Lightly grease baking sheets. In a medium bowl, combine GINGERBREAD MIX, molasses, egg and flour. Blend well. On a lightly floured surface, roll out to ¼-inch thickness. Cut into gingerbread boy shapes, about 6 inches long. Place on prepared baking sheets. Bake 10 to 12 minutes, until edges are browned. When cooled, brush on Icing Glaze with a clean new ½-inch paintbrush. Decorate as desired. Makes about 12 gingerbread boys.

Icing Glaze:

Combine ingredients in a small bowl. Stir until smooth. Thin with water, if necessary, to reach consistency for brushing.

How to Make A Gingerbread House

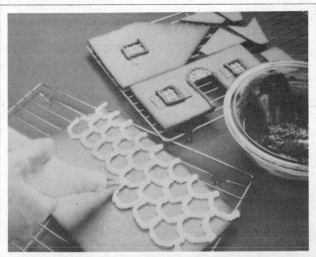

1/Use Icing Mortar to decorate the house pieces
as desired. Let each piece dry 3 to 4 hours.

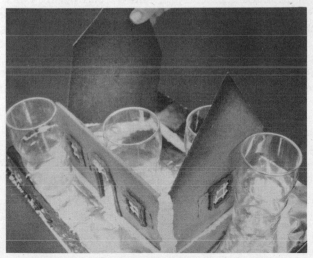

2/Stand the walls of the house in a row of Icing Mortar
and prop them with glasses to keep them straight.

Sugar Cookies

Delightfully tasty any way you bake 'em!

3 cups QUICK MIX,
   page 15
1 cup sugar
½ cup milk or water

1 egg, slightly beaten
1 teaspoon vanilla, lemon
   or almond extract

Preheat oven to 375°F (190°C). Lightly grease baking sheets. Combine QUICK MIX and sugar in a medium bowl. Blend well. In a small bowl, combine milk or water, egg and extract. Add to dry ingredients. Blend well. Drop by teaspoonfuls onto prepared baking sheets. Bake 10 to 12 minutes until lightly browned. Makes 30 to 36 cookies.

Variations

Flavor Drop Cookies: Add 1 cup nuts, raisins, small gumdrops, chocolate chips, butterscotch chips or dates. For coconut cookies, add 1½ cups shredded coconut. For peanut butter cookies, add ½ cup peanut butter. For orange cookies, omit extract and add 1 tablespoon orange peel and ½ cup raisins. For molasses cookies, substitute 3 tablespoons molasses for milk or water and add ⅛ teaspoon mace.

Shaped Cookies: Decrease milk or water to 3 tablespoons. Shape dough into 1-inch balls. Place about 3 inches apart on prepared baking sheets. Flatten each ball with the bottom of a glass dipped in sugar.

Rolled Cookies: Decrease milk or water to 3 tablespoons. On a lightly floured surface, roll out dough to ⅛-inch thickness. Sprinkle with sugar and cut into shapes. Place about 1 inch apart on prepared baking sheets.

Very Vanilla Cookies

Delicious in any flavor.

3 cups BASIC COOKIE MIX, page 32	1½ teaspoons vanilla
	1 egg
1 teaspoon milk, more if necessary	Sugar or frosting, if desired

Preheat oven to 375°F (190°C). Lightly grease baking sheets. In a large bowl, combine BASIC COOKIE MIX, milk, vanilla and egg. Blend well. Drop by teaspoonfuls onto prepared baking sheets. Sprinkle with sugar, if desired. Bake 10 to 15 minutes, until edges are golden. Frost, if desired. Makes about 24 cookies.

Variations

Spice Vanilla Cookies: Add 2 teaspoons pumpkin pie spice and ½ cup nuts to dough.
Cocoa Cookies: Add 2 tablespoons cocoa and increase milk to 2 tablespoons. Frost, if desired.
Holiday Pinwheels: Divide dough in half. Color half green and half red. Cover each half with wax paper and roll out to rectangles of equal size. Remove wax paper. Place one rectangle on top of the other and roll like a jelly roll. Chill 2 to 3 hours. Cut into ⅛-inch slices.

Chocolate Chip Cookies

The rich flavor of chocolate chips in every bite.

3 cups BASIC COOKIE MIX, page 32	1 egg
	½ cup nuts or coconut
1 tablespoon milk, more if necessary	1 cup chocolate chips or sugar-coated chocolate candies
1 teaspoon vanilla	

Preheat oven to 375°F (190°C). Grease baking sheets. In a large bowl, combine BASIC COOKIE MIX, milk, vanilla and egg. Blend well. Stir in nuts or coconut and chocolate chips or candies. Drop by teaspoonfuls onto prepared baking sheets. Bake 10 to 15 minutes, until golden brown. Makes about 24 cookies.

Chewy Chocolate Cookies

Crown each one with a nut.

2 eggs, slightly beaten	½ teaspoon baking soda
¼ cup water	¾ cup flour
2¼ cups BROWNIE	1 teaspoon vanilla
MIX, page 36	Walnut or pecan halves

Preheat oven to 375°F (190°C). Butter baking sheets. Combine eggs and water in a medium bowl. Beat with a fork until blended. Stir in BROWNIE MIX, baking soda, flour and vanilla. Blend well. Drop by teaspoonfuls 2 inches apart on prepared baking sheets. Put a walnut or pecan half in center of each cookie. Bake 10 to 12 minutes, until edges are browned. Cool on wire racks. Makes about 36 cookies.

Sweet & Spicy Cookies

This cookie is as popular with children as adults.

2 cups BASIC COOKIE	½ teaspoon ginger
MIX, page 32	½ teaspoon cinnamon
4 tablespoons molasses	½ teaspoon allspice
½ teaspoon vanilla	Sugar
1 egg, beaten	

Preheat oven to 375°F (190°C). Lightly grease baking sheets. In a medium bowl, combine BASIC COOKIE MIX, molasses, vanilla, egg, ginger, cinnamon and allspice. Stir until blended. Drop by teaspoonfuls 2 inches apart on prepared baking sheets. Flatten with the bottom of a glass dipped in sugar. Bake 8 to

10 minutes, until edges are browned. Makes about 24 cookies.

Peanut Butter & Honey Cookies

A favorite flavor combination makes these special.

2 cups OATMEAL
  COOKIE MIX,
  pages 32–33
½ cup chunky-style
  peanut butter

⅓ cup honey
½ teaspoon vanilla

Preheat oven to 375°F (190°C). Lightly grease baking sheets. Combine all ingredients in a medium bowl. Blend well. Drop by teaspoonfuls 2 inches apart on prepared baking sheets. Bake 10 to 12 minutes, until edges are browned. Makes about 30 cookies.

Spice-Raisin Cookies

Super for a mid-day snack.

6 cups OATMEAL
  COOKIE MIX,
  pages 32–33
2 eggs, beaten
½ cup milk

1 teaspoon cinnamon
½ teaspoon nutmeg
½ teaspoon cloves
1 cup raisins
½ cup chopped nuts

Preheat oven to 350°F (175°C). Lightly grease baking sheets. Put OATMEAL COOKIE MIX in a large bowl. Add eggs, milk, cinnamon, nutmeg and cloves. Blend well. Stir in raisins and nuts. Drop by teaspoonfuls 2 inches apart on prepared baking sheets. Bake 12 to 15 minutes, until edges are browned. Makes about 48 cookies.

Gumdrop Jewels

Kids love the rainbow colors.

2 cups OATMEAL
  COOKIE MIX,
  pages 32–33
1 egg, beaten

2 tablespoons milk
½ cup shredded coconut
1 cup chopped, fruit-
  flavored gumdrops

Preheat oven to 375°F (190°C). Lightly grease baking sheets. In a medium bowl, combine OATMEAL COOKIE MIX, egg and milk. Blend well. Stir in coconut and gumdrops. Drop by teaspoonfuls onto prepared baking sheets. Bake 10 to 12 minutes, until edges are browned. Makes about 30 cookies.

Oatmeal Cookies

Crisp and crunchy with a sweet oatmeal flavor.

¼ cup milk
1 teaspoon vanilla
1 egg
3 cups OATMEAL
  MIX, pages 32–33

½ teaspoon cinnamon
¼ teaspoon cloves
½ cup raisins

Preheat oven to 350°F (175°C). Lightly grease baking sheets. In a small bowl, combine milk, vanilla and egg. Put OATMEAL MIX, cinnamon and cloves in a medium bowl. Add liquid ingredients all at once and stir until just blended. Stir in raisins. Drop by teaspoonfuls onto prepared baking sheets. Bake 10 to 15 minutes, until edges are browned. Cool cookies on wire racks. Makes about 24 cookies.

Variation

For a milder cookie, omit cinnamon and cloves.

Oatmeal Chippers

If you love both oatmeal and chocolate chips, start baking!

2 eggs, beaten
½ cup milk
2 teaspoons vanilla
6 cups OATMEAL
COOKIE MIX,
pages 32–33

1 (6-oz.) pkg. semisweet
chocolate chips
½ cup chopped nuts

Preheat oven to 350°F (175°C). Lightly grease baking sheets. In a large bowl, combine eggs, milk, vanilla and OATMEAL COOKIE MIX. Add chocolate chips and nuts. Drop by teaspoonfuls 2 inches apart on prepared baking sheets. Bake 12 to 15 minutes, until edges are browned. Makes about 48 cookies.

Breakfast Cookies

Add extra nutrition to your cookies.

½ cup shortening
1 cup brown sugar,
firmly packed
2 eggs
1 tablespoon milk
1 teaspoon vanilla

1¼ cups all-purpose
flour
½ teaspoon baking soda
¼ teaspoon salt
2 cups GRANOLA MIX,
pages 33–34

Preheat oven to 350°F (175°C). Lightly grease baking sheets. Cream together shortening and brown sugar in a large bowl. Add eggs, milk and vanilla. Beat well. In a medium bowl, combine flour, baking soda and salt. Mix well and add to sugar mixture. Stir in GRANOLA MIX. Drop by teaspoonfuls onto prepared baking sheets. Bake 10 to 12 minutes, until edges are browned. Makes about 36 cookies.

Tropic Macaroons

A South Seas adventure in cookies.

2 cups BASIC COOKIE
   MIX, page 32
2 egg yolks
1 (8½-oz.) can crushed
   pineapple, drained

1¼ cups shredded coco-
   nut, more if desired
Maraschino cherries, for
   garnish

Preheat oven to 350°F (175°C). Lightly grease baking sheets. In a medium bowl, combine BASIC COOKIE MIX, egg yolks, pineapple and coconut. Stir until well-blended. Drop by teaspoonfuls onto prepared baking sheets. Top with maraschino cherries. Bake 12 to 15 minutes, until edges are golden. Makes 30 to 36 cookies.

Banana-Coconut Delights

Make these giant-size and serve for
breakfast with a glass of milk.

2 cups BASIC COOKIE
   MIX, page 32
1 cup flaked coconut
1 medium banana,
   mashed

1 teaspoon vanilla
1 egg, beaten
½ cup chopped nuts
½ cup rolled oats

Preheat oven to 375°F (190°C). Lightly grease baking sheets. In a medium bowl, combine BASIC COOKIE MIX, coconut, banana, vanilla and egg. Beat well. Stir in chopped nuts and oats. Drop by teaspoonfuls onto prepared baking sheets. Bake 10 to 12 minutes, until edges are browned. Makes about 36 cookies.

Date-Filled Drop Cookies

An old-fashioned favorite made easy.

Date Filling, see below
4 cups BASIC COOKIE MIX, page 32
¼ teaspoon cinnamon
2 eggs, beaten
1 teaspoon vanilla
¼ cup water or buttermilk
Walnut halves

Date Filling:

1 cup chopped dates
3 tablespoons sugar
3 tablespoons water
¼ cup chopped nuts

Prepare Date Filling and set aside to cool. Preheat oven to 375°F (190°C). Lightly grease baking sheets. In a large bowl, combine BASIC COOKIE MIX, cinnamon, eggs, vanilla and water or buttermilk. Blend well. Drop by teaspoonfuls onto prepared baking sheets. Spoon ½ teaspoon Date Filling on top of each cookie, depressing dough slightly. Cover each with another teaspoon of dough. Top with walnut half. Bake 10 to 12 minutes, until browned. Makes 30 to 36 cookies.

Date Filling:

In a small saucepan, combine dates, sugar and water. Cook over medium heat about 5 to 10 minutes, stirring, until thick. Remove from heat. Cool slightly. Stir in chopped nuts.

Variation

Raisin-filled Drop Cookies: Substitute raisins for dates.

It's easy to overbake cookies, so remove them from the oven just before you think they're done, and remove them from the baking sheets immediately so they do not continue cooking.

Snappy Ginger Cookies

*The combination of gingerbread
and molasses makes a real treat.*

3 cups GINGERBREAD   1 egg
   MIX, page 31   Sugar
⅓ cup molasses

Preheat oven to 350°F (175°C). Lightly grease baking sheets. In a medium bowl, combine GINGERBREAD MIX, molasses and egg. Blend well. Chill dough for easier handling, if desired. Shape into 1-inch balls. Roll in sugar. Place balls 2 inches apart on prepared baking sheets. Flatten balls with bottom of a small glass. Bake 12 to 15 minutes, until edges are browned. Makes about 24 cookies.

Variation

Roll balls in mixture of 1 teaspoon cinnamon and 3 tablespoons sugar before flattening.

Molasses Cookies

Soft and chewy.

2 cups QUICK MIX,   ¼ teaspoon cloves
   page 15   1 egg yolk
¼ cup sugar   ½ cup molasses
½ teaspoon cinnamon   Sugar
½ teaspoon ginger

In a medium bowl, combine QUICK MIX, ¼ cup sugar, cinnamon, ginger and cloves. Mix well. Combine egg yolk and molasses in a small bowl. Add to dry mixture. Blend well. Refrigerate at least one hour. Preheat oven to 375°F (190°C). Lightly grease baking sheets. Shape dough into 1½-inch balls, and roll in sugar. Place on prepared baking sheets. Flatten balls with the bottom of a glass dipped in sugar. Bake 8 to 10 minutes, until edges are browned. Makes about 30 cookies.

Cinnamon Thins

The thinnner the better!

3 cups QUICK MIX,
  page 15
2 tablespoons sugar
¼ cup butter or mar-
  garine, melted

½ cup milk or water
1 egg, well beaten
1⅓ cups sugar
3 tablespoons cinnamon

Preheat oven to 450°F (230°C). Generously grease
baking sheets. In a medium bowl, combine QUICK
MIX and 2 tablespoons sugar. Stir until well-blended.
In a small bowl, combine melted butter or margarine,
milk or water and egg. Add to dry ingredients. Stir with
a fork until mixture is moistened. On a lightly floured
surface, knead 8 to 10 times, until dough is smooth.
Form dough into forty 1-inch balls. Mix together 1⅓
cups sugar and cinnamon and sprinkle generously on
wax paper. Coat each ball with sugar-cinnamon mixture. Place another sheet of wax paper on top of ball.
Roll with a rolling pin, turning dough over several
times until well-coated and paper thin. Place on prepared baking sheets. Bake about 4 to 5 minutes, until
light brown and crisp. Makes 40 thins.

Snickerdoodles

Soft when they're warm and snappy when they're cool!

2½ cups BASIC
  COOKIE MIX,
  page 32
¼ teaspoon baking soda
1 teaspoon cream of
  tartar

1 egg
2 tablespoons sugar
1 teaspoon cinnamon

Preheat oven to 400°F (205°C). In medium bowl,
combine BASIC COOKIE MIX, baking soda, cream of
tartar and egg. Mix well. Combine sugar and cinnamon

in a small dish. Shape dough into 1½-inch balls. Roll in sugar-cinnamon mixture and place 2 inches apart on unbuttered baking sheets. Flatten balls slightly. Bake 8 to 10 minutes, until lightly browned with cracked tops. Makes about 30 cookies.

Peanut Butter Cookies

A better peanut butter batter.

3 cups BASIC COOKIE MIX, page 32	1 teaspoon vanilla
¼ cup brown sugar, firmly packed	2 eggs
	½ cup chunky-style peanut butter

Preheat oven to 375°F (190°C). Lightly grease baking sheets. Combine all ingredients in a medium bowl. Blend well. Shape dough into 1-inch balls. Place on prepared baking sheets and flatten with fork tines. Bake 10 to 12 minutes, until edges are browned. Makes 30 to 36 cookies.

Variation

Peanut Butter & Jelly Cookies: On baking sheets, press thumb into center of balls. Do not flatten. Fill with grape jelly.

Don't crowd cookies on your baking sheets, as this may cause uneven coloring during baking.

Crescent Butter Cookies

So good they melt in your mouth.

2 cups QUICK MIX,
   page 15
¼ cup granulated sugar
½ cup butter

1 teaspoon vanilla
½ cup chopped pecans
   or walnuts
Powdered sugar

Preheat oven to 350°F (175°C). In a medium bowl, combine QUICK MIX and granulated sugar. Mix well. With a pastry blender, cut in butter until evenly distributed. Add vanilla and nuts. Blend well. Roll teaspoonfuls of dough to thin, 2½-inch lengths. Shape into crescents on unbuttered baking sheets. Bake 8 to 10 minutes, until light brown. Cool slightly. Roll warm cookies in powdered sugar. Makes 36 to 48 cookies.

Variation

Add ¼ cup finely chopped dates to dough before shaping.
Shape dough into 1-inch balls, if preferred.

How to Make Crescent Butter Cookies

1/Roll teaspoonfuls of dough to about ⅜-inch widths, about 2½ inches long. Shape into crescents on unbuttered baking sheets.

2/Bake the crescents until light brown. While still warm, coat each with powdered sugar.

Lemon-Nut Icebox Cookies

A light, refreshing cookie.

1 egg yolk
1 tablespoon milk
1 teaspoon grated lemon
  peel
1/8 teaspoon almond
  flavoring

2 cups BASIC COOKIE
  MIX, page 32
1/3 cup chopped nuts

In a medium bowl, combine egg yolk, milk, grated lemon peel and almond flavoring. Add BASIC COOKIE MIX and nuts. Shape into a long, 2-inch-diameter roll. Cover with plastic wrap and refrigerate 3 to 4 hours or overnight. Preheat oven to 375°F (190°C). Cut roll into 1/8-inch slices. Bake on unbuttered baking sheets 8 to 10 minutes, until edges are golden. Cool on wire racks. Makes about 36 cookies.

Variation

Chocolate-Nut Icebox Cookies: Omit lemon peel and almond flavoring. Add 1/2 teaspoon vanilla and 1 (1-oz.) square unsweetened chocolate, melted.

Spicebox Cookies

They're ready when you are.

2 cups BASIC COOKIE
  MIX, page 32
1 egg
1/4 teaspoon baking soda
1/4 teaspoon cinnamon

1/4 teaspoon cloves
1/4 teaspoon allspice
1/4 teaspoon vanilla
1/2 cup chopped nuts

In a medium bowl, combine BASIC COOKIE MIX, egg, baking soda, cinnamon, cloves, allspice and vanilla. Mix well. Stir in chopped nuts. Shape into a long, 2-inch-diameter roll. Cover with plastic wrap and refrigerate 3 to 4 hours or overnight. Preheat oven to

375°F (190°C). Lightly grease baking sheets. Cut roll into ⅛-inch slices and place on prepared baking sheets. Bake 8 to 10 minutes, until edges are golden brown. Cool on wire racks. Makes about 30 cookies.

Our Best Brownies

A delightful, chewy treat.

2 eggs, beaten	½ cup chopped nuts
1 teaspoon vanilla	Brownie Toppers, see
2½ cups BROWNIE MIX, page 36	below

Preheat oven to 350°F (175°C). Grease and flour an 8-inch square pan. In a medium bowl, combine eggs, vanilla and BROWNIE MIX. Beat until smooth. Stir in nuts. Pour into prepared pan. Bake 30 to 35 minutes, until edges separate from pan. Cool. Cut into 2-inch bars. Sprinkle or frost with Brownie Topper of your choice. Makes 16 brownies.

Variation

For cake-like brownies, add 2 tablespoons milk to batter.

Brownie Toppers:

Powdered Sugar Sprinkle: Sprinkle warm brownies with powdered sugar.

Chocolate Topper: Sprinkle contents of 1 (6-oz.) package chocolate chips over warm brownies. Warm in oven until melted. Spread evenly on brownies. Sprinkle with chopped nuts, if desired.

Chocolate Mint Topper: Spread contents of 1 (5½-oz.) package chocolate-covered mints over warm brownies. Warm in oven until melted. Spread evenly on brownies.

Marshmallow Surprise: Prepare ½ recipe Cocoa Icing, page 208. Sprinkle 1½ cups miniature marshmallows over warm brownies. Warm in oven until melted, about 2 to 3 minutes. Frost with Cocoa Icing.

Bittersweet Frosting: In a small saucepan, combine 1½ cups powdered sugar, ½ cup butter or margarine and ½ cup evaporated milk. Cook over medium-high heat about 7 to 10 minutes, until temperature reaches 230°F (110°C). Cool mixture. Beat until stiff and spread on brownies. In a small saucepan, melt 2 (1-oz.) squares unsweetened chocolate over low heat, and spread over topping.

Coconut-Pecan Topping: In a small saucepan, combine ⅓ cup sugar, ⅓ cup evaporated milk, 1 beaten egg yolk and 3 tablespoons butter or margarine. Cook over medium heat about 5 minutes, stirring constantly, until mixture comes to a boil. Remove from heat and stir in ¼ teaspoon vanilla, ⅔ cup flaked coconut and ½ cup chopped pecans. Cool 10 minutes. Spread on cooled brownies.

> *To cut gumdrops, use a pair of scissors dipped in flour.*

Millionaire Bars

So rich you won't believe it!

1 (14-oz.) pkg. caramels
⅓ cup evaporated milk
2½ cups QUICK MIX, page 15
⅓ cup cocoa
¾ cup granulated sugar
½ cup brown sugar, firmly packed
½ cup butter or margarine, melted
⅓ cup evaporated milk
1 (6-oz.) pkg. chocolate chips
¾ cup chopped nuts

Preheat oven to 350°F (175°C). Lightly grease and flour a 13″ × 9″ baking pan. In a medium saucepan, combine caramels and ⅓ cup evaporated milk. Cook over low heat about 10 minutes, stirring constantly until caramels are melted. Keep warm. In a medium bowl, combine QUICK MIX, cocoa, granulated sugar, brown sugar, butter or margarine and ⅓ cup evaporated milk. Stir until dough holds together. Press half of dough into prepared pan, reserving remaining dough for topping. Bake about 7 minutes, until edges are browned. Remove from oven and cool slightly. Drizzle caramel mixture evenly over baked crust and sprinkle with chocolate chips and nuts. Top with remaining dough. Bake 15 to 20 more minutes, until edges separate from pan. Cool thoroughly. Cut into 2-inch squares. Makes about 24 to 30 bars:

Caramelita Oatmeal Bars

The caramel filling makes them irresistible.

Caramel Filling, see below
3½ cups OATMEAL MIX, pages 18–19
½ cup sugar
½ cup butter or margarine, melted
1 (6-oz.) pkg. chocolate chips
½ cup chopped nuts

Caramel Filling:

1 (14-oz.) pkg. caramels   ¼ cup evaporated milk

Prepare Caramel Filling and keep warm. Preheat oven to 350°F (175°C). Combine OATMEAL MIX and sugar in a large bowl. Add melted butter or margarine. Press half of mixture into an unbuttered 13″ × 9″ baking pan. Bake about 10 minutes, until edges are browned. Sprinkle chocolate chips and nuts over oatmeal layer. Drizzle Caramel Filling evenly over chocolate chips and nuts. Sprinkle remaining oatmeal mixture over top. Press down slightly. Bake 15 more minutes, until edges are browned. Cool thoroughly. Cut into 2-inch squares. Makes about 24 to 30 bars.

Caramel Filling:

In a medium saucepan, melt caramels with evaporated milk. Cook over low heat about 5 to 10 minutes, stirring constantly, until caramels are melted.

Magic Granola Bars

They disappear like magic!

½ cup butter or margarine
1½ cups crushed graham crackers
1⅓ cups flaked coconut
¾ cup chocolate chips
¾ cup butterscotch chips
1 cup GRANOLA MIX, pages 33–34
1 (15-oz.) can sweetened condensed milk

Preheat oven to 350°F (175°C). Put butter or margarine in a 13″ × 9″ baking pan. Melt in preheating oven. Sprinkle crushed graham crackers evenly over melted butter or margarine. Sprinkle coconut evenly over crumbs. In a small bowl, combine chocolate chips and butterscotch chips. Sprinkle over coconut. Sprinkle with GRANOLA MIX. Drizzle with sweetened condensed milk. Bake about 25 minutes, until edges are browned. Cool. Cut into 2-inch squares. Makes about 24 to 30 squares.

Fruit Bar Cookies

You get a choice of fillings!

Apricot Filling, see below
2½ cups OATMEAL
   MIX, pages 18–19

½ cup sugar
¼ cup butter or marga-
   rine, melted

Apricot Filling:

1½ cups chopped dried
   apricots
½ cup brown sugar,
   firmly packed

1 cup water
1 teaspoon lemon juice
¾ cup flaked coconut

Prepare Apricot Filling. Preheat oven to 375°F
(190°C). Lightly grease an 8-inch square pan. Combine OATMEAL MIX and sugar in a medium bowl.
Add melted butter or margarine. Press half of oatmeal
mixture onto bottom of prepared pan. Spread filling
over oatmeal layer. Crumble remaining oatmeal mixture over top. Bake about 30 minutes, until browned.
Cool thoroughly. Cut into 2-inch bars. Makes 16 bars.

Apricot Filling:

In a small saucepan, combine apricots, brown sugar,
water and lemon juice. Cook over low heat about 10
minutes, stirring frequently until thickened. Stir in coconut. Cool.

Variation

Date Filling: Omit Apricot Filling. In a small saucepan, combine 1 cup chopped pitted dates, ½ cup sugar,
¼ cup orange juice and ¾ cup water. Cook over low
heat about 10 to 15 minutes, stirring frequently, until
thickened. Cool.

CAKES

Cakes are always a popular dessert, whether unadorned or decorated to suit the occasion. Guests who drop in will be amazed at the speed with which you can create a cake from your Master Mixes. You will find great enjoyment in serving cakes made from ingredients which are fresh and free of preservatives. Most of the cakes come from BASIC CAKE MIX, but you will also delight at the Caramel-Nut Pudding Cake and Pineapple Upside-Down Cake made from QUICK MIX. There are even cake recipes using MUFFIN MIX, GINGERBREAD MIX and BROWNIE MIX.

Mixing procedures play a big role in producing high-quality cakes. Measure cake ingredients accurately, using ingredients at room temperature. Cakes are better when the batter is beaten with an electric mixer 3 to 4 minutes. If you overbeat, the fat will separate, causing a poor-quality cake. For a velvety texture, the cake batter should be at least 1-inch deep in the pan. When using BASIC CAKE MIX, it is important to add a portion of the liquid first to make a smooth batter. Then add the remaining ingredients, and mix.

Grandma's Picnic Cake is unique. The light texture and blend of brown sugar, nuts and chocolate chips in the topping appeal to anyone's appetite on an outing. Mom's Spumoni Cake is superb for an extra-special occasion. The assortment of flavors and colors makes it delicious and beautiful. And no one can resist Chocolate-Nut Torte, a party adaptation of Irresistible Chocolate Cake.

Most cakes can be frozen before frosting, but they dry out rapidly after thawing. Remember, with your own mixes, you can bake just the amount you need. Half portions are a snap!

HIGH ALTITUDE BAKING

Many baked products tend to fall or give unpredictable results in altitudes over 3,000 feet above sea level. There are 3 basic adjustments you can make to correct this in cakes:

- Increase the liquid 1 to 2 tablespoons at 3,000 feet, 2 to 3 tablespoons at 5,000 feet, or 3 to 4 tablespoons at 7,000 feet for each cup of liquid called for in the recipe.
- Decrease the baking powder ⅛ teaspoon at 3,000 feet, ⅛ to ¼ teaspoon at 5,000 feet, or ¼ teaspoon at 7,000 feet for each teaspoon called for.
- Decrease the sugar up to 1 tablespoon at 3,000 feet, up to 2 tablespoons at 5,000 feet, or 1 to 3 tablespoons at 7,000 feet for each cup called for.

Be sure to adjust all 3 ingredients. Because each recipe is different, experiment to discover the best proportions. Try a smaller amount first, then add more if necessary.

Apple-Nut Cake

A spicy snackin' cake.

2⅓ cups QUICK MIX,
   page 15
1 cup brown sugar,
   firmly packed
1 teaspoon cinnamon
½ teaspoon cloves

2 eggs, slightly beaten
¼ cup milk or water
2 cups pared, cored and
   grated apples
½ cup raisins
½ cup chopped nuts

Preheat oven to 375°F (190°C). Lightly grease an 8-inch square pan. In a medium bowl, combine QUICK MIX, brown sugar, cinnamon and cloves. Mix well. Add eggs and milk or water. Blend with electric mixer 1 minute. Add apples and blend 2 more minutes. Stir in raisins and nuts. Pour into prepared pan. Bake 40 to 50 minutes, until a toothpick inserted in center comes out clean. Cool in pan 10 minutes, then cool on a wire rack. Makes one 8-inch cake.

Variation

Banana-Nut Cake: Omit raisins. Substitute 1 cup mashed bananas for apples.

Buttermilk-Chocolate Cake

Buttermilk gives it a lighter texture.

3⅓ cups BASIC CAKE
  MIX, page 30
½ cup sugar
2 eggs, beaten
1 cup buttermilk

½ cup cocoa
½ cup boiling water
1 teaspoon baking soda
1 teaspoon vanilla

Creamy Frosting:

1 cup milk
2 tablespoons flour
Pinch of salt
½ cup butter or marga-
  rine, room temperature

½ cup vegetable shorten-
  ing, room temperature
1 cup granulated sugar
1 teaspoon vanilla

Preheat oven to 350°F (175°C). Lightly grease and flour two 8-inch, round pans. In a large bowl, combine BASIC CAKE MIX, sugar, eggs and buttermilk. Mix well. In a small bowl, mix togther cocoa, boiling water, baking soda and vanilla. Add to the cake mixture. Beat well. Pour into prepared pans. Bake 10 minutes. Turn oven to 375°F (190°C) and bake 20 more minutes, until a toothpick inserted in center comes out clean. Cool in pans 20 minutes, then cool on a wire rack. Prepare Creamy Frosting. Frost cooled cake. Makes one 2-layer cake.

Creamy Frosting:

Cook together milk, flour and salt about 5 minutes, until thickened. Cool. Combine butter or margarine, shortening and sugar in a small bowl. Beat well. Add to cooled milk mixture, beating constantly. Beat about 7 minutes until smooth. Stir in vanilla. Makes about 3 cups frosting.

Mom's Spumoni Cake

This prize winner is a delightful blend of flavors and colors.

Rainbow Frosting, see below
3⅓ cups BASIC CAKE MIX, page 30
½ cup sugar
2 eggs, beaten

1 cup buttermilk
½ cup cocoa
½ cup boiling water
1 teaspoon baking soda
1 teaspoon vanilla

Rainbow Frosting:

1 cup milk
2 tablespoons flour
Pinch of salt
½ cup butter or margarine, room temperature
½ cup vegetable shortening, room temperature
1 cup granulated sugar
2 to 3 drops green food coloring
¼ teaspoon almond flavoring

2 to 3 drops yellow food coloring
¼ teaspoon lemon flavoring
2 to 3 drops red food coloring
¼ teaspoon peppermint flavoring
3 tablespoons cocoa
¼ teaspoon vanilla

Prepare Rainbow Frosting and set aside. Preheat oven to 350°F (175°C). Grease and lightly flour two 8-inch, round pans. In a large bowl, combine BASIC CAKE MIX, sugar, eggs and buttermilk. Mix well. In a small bowl, mix together cocoa, boiling water, baking soda and vanilla. Add cocoa mixture to cake mixture. Beat well. Pour into prepared pans. Bake 10 minutes. Turn oven to 375°F (190°C) and bake 20 more minutes, until a toothpick inserted in center comes out clean. Cool in pans 10 minutes, then cool on wire racks. Cut each cake with a serrated knife to make 2 layers each. Frost each layer with a different color of Rainbow Frosting. Stack layers. Do not frost sides. Makes one 4-layer cake.

Rainbow Frosting:

In a small saucepan, combine milk, flour and salt. Cook over medium heat about 5 to 7 minutes, until thickened. Cool. Combine butter or margarine, shortening and sugar in a medium bowl. Beat well. Add to cooled milk mixture, beating constantly. Beat about 7 minutes, until smooth. Divide mixture among 4 bowls. In the first bowl, add green food coloring and almond flavoring. In the second bowl, add yellow food coloring and lemon flavoring. In a third bowl, add red food coloring and peppermint flavoring. Add cocoa and vanilla to the fourth bowl.

Irresistible Chocolate Cake

Rich! Fill the house with this aroma!

3⅓ cups BASIC CAKE MIX, page 30
9 tablespoons cocoa
1 cup milk
2 eggs, well-beaten
2½ tablespoons butter or margarine, melted
Fudge Sauce, pages 215–216, or frosting, as desired

Preheat oven to 375°F (190°C). Lightly grease and flour two 8-inch, round pans. Combine BASIC CAKE MIX and cocoa in a large bowl. Add ½ cup of the milk and beat at medium speed for 2 minutes. Add remaining ½ cup milk, eggs and melted butter or margarine. Beat 2 more minutes. Pour into prepared pans. Bake 25 to 30 minutes, until a toothpick inserted in center comes out clean. Cool in pans 10 minutes, then cool on wire racks. Top with Fudge Sauce, or frost as desired. Makes one 2-layer cake.

Chocolate-Nut Torte

Elegance simplified!

Torte Topping, see below
3⅓ cups BASIC CAKE
  MIX, page 30
9 tablespoons cocoa
1 cup milk

2 eggs, well beaten
2½ tablespoons butter or
  margarine, melted
½ pint whipping cream,
  whipped and sweetened

Torte Topping:

½ cup butter or margarine
1 cup brown sugar,
  firmly packed

1 cup chopped nuts

Prepare Torte Topping and set aside. Preheat oven to 350°F (175°C). Lightly grease four 8-inch, round cake pans. Line pans with wax paper. Butter wax paper. Divide Torte Topping evenly among 4 cake pans. In a large bowl, combine BASIC CAKE MIX and cocoa. Add ½ cup of milk and beat at medium speed 2 minutes. Add remaining ½ cup milk, eggs and melted butter or margarine. Beat 2 more minutes. Pour batter over Torte Topping in cake pans. Bake 15 to 20 minutes, until a toothpick inserted in center comes out clean. Cool in pans 10 minutes. Cool slightly on wire racks, and peel off wax paper. Cool thoroughly. Stack and frost with whipped cream between layers and on top. Do not frost sides. Makes 1 torte.

Torte Topping:

Melt butter or margarine in a small skillet over medium heat. Stir in brown sugar and nuts.

Hot Fudge Pudding Cake

Chocolate cake on top and a fudgy
pudding sauce below. Serve it a la mode!

1½ cups QUICK MIX,
    page 15
½ cup granulated sugar
2 tablespoons cocoa
¾ cup chopped nuts
½ cup milk

1 teaspoon vanilla
¾ cup brown sugar,
    firmly packed
¼ cup cocoa
1½ cups boiling water

Preheat oven to 350°F (175°C). In an unbuttered, 8-inch square pan, combine QUICK MIX, granulated sugar, 2 tablespoons cocoa, nuts, milk and vanilla. Blend well. Combine brown sugar and ¼ cup cocoa in a small bowl. Sprinkle over top of cake mixture. Gently pour boiling water over top of mixture. Do not stir. Bake 35 to 40 minutes, until edges separate from pan. Cool in pan 15 minutes before serving. Makes one 8-inch cake.

Variation
Omit nuts and add 1 cup miniature marshmallows.

Caramel-Nut Pudding Cake

Delicate cake and scrumptious
caramel pudding—what a combination!

1 cup QUICK MIX,
    page 15
½ cup brown sugar,
    firmly packed
½ cup raisins, if desired

½ cup chopped nuts
½ cup milk
Brown Sugar Topping,
    see below

Brown Sugar Topping:

1 cup brown sugar,
    firmly packed
1 tablespoon butter or
    margarine

2 cups boiling water

Preheat oven to 375°F (190°C). Lightly grease an 8-inch square pan. In a medium bowl, combine QUICK MIX, brown sugar, raisins, if desired, and nuts. Mix well. Add milk and blend well. Pour into prepared pan. Prepare Brown Sugar Topping. Gently pour over top of cake mixture without stirring. Bake 30 to 40 minutes, until cake springs back when lightly touched in center. Cool in pan 15 minutes before serving. Makes one 8-inch cake.

Brown Sugar Topping:

In a small bowl, combine brown sugar, butter or margarine and boiling water. Blend.

Cherry Dessert Cake

A speedy-to-make and luscious-to-eat dessert.

2 (21-oz.) cans cherry pie filling
3⅓ cups BASIC CAKE MIX, page 30

1 cup butter or margarine, melted
1 (3-oz.) pkg. slivered almonds

Preheat oven to 350°F (175°C). Pour cherry pie filling into a 13″ × 9″ pan. Sprinkle BASIC CAKE MIX on top of pie filling. Drizzle melted butter or margarine over top of mix. Top with slivered almonds. Bake about 45 minutes, until lightly browned. Cool in pan. Makes one large cake.

If you have trouble removing cakes from pans, butter the pan, line it with wax paper, then butter the wax paper. Remove the wax paper immediately after turning the cake out of the pan.

Cinnamon-Nut Bundt Cake

This cake's excellent texture is enhanced by a nut filling.

Nut filling, see below
3½ cups BASIC CAKE
  MIX, page 30
1 (4-oz.) pkg. instant
  vanilla pudding

½ cup vegetable oil
1 cup milk
4 eggs
Vanilla Frosting, see
  below

Nut Filling:

¼ cup sugar
2 teaspoons cinnamon

½ cup coarsely chopped
  nuts

Vanilla Frosting:

1 cup sifted powdered
  sugar

½ teaspoon vanilla
1½ tablespoons milk

Preheat oven to 375°F (190°C). Generously grease and flour a bundt pan. Prepare Nut Filling. In a large bowl, combine BASIC CAKE MIX, vanilla pudding, oil and milk. Beat with electric mixer about 4 minutes. Add eggs 1 at a time, beating well after each. Pour one-third of cake batter into prepared pan. Sprinkle with half of Nut Filling, then another third of cake batter. Sprinkle remaining Nut Filling and remaining batter over top. Bake 40 to 45 minutes, until a toothpick inserted in center comes out clean. Cool in pan 10 minutes, then cool on a wire rack. Prepare Vanilla Frosting and frost cooled cake. Makes 1 bundt cake.

Nut Filling:

Combine ingredients in a small bowl. Mix well.

Vanilla Frosting:

Combine powdered sugar and vanilla in a small bowl. Gradually add milk to make a medium-thin frosting.

Cranberry Cakes

Sweet, tart & irresistible!

1 cup raw whole
  cranberries
½ cup sugar
2⅓ cups MUFFIN MIX,
  page 18

1 cup evaporated milk
1 tablespoon butter or
  margarine, melted
Hot Butter Sauce,
  page 210

Preheat oven to 400°F (205°C). Generously grease muffin pans. In a small bowl, combine cranberries and sugar and let stand a few minutes. Put MUFFIN MIX in a medium bowl. Add evaporated milk and melted butter or margarine to sweetened cranberries. Add cranberry mixture all at once to MUFFIN MIX. Stir until just moistened; batter should be lumpy. Fill prepared muffin pans half full. Bake 15 to 20 minutes, until golden brown. Serve warm with Hot Butter Sauce. Makes about 24 cakes.

Elegant White Cake

So basically good, it has many uses.

3⅓ cups BASIC CAKE
  MIX, page 30
¾ cup milk

3 egg whites
1 teaspoon vanilla
Frosting, as desired

Preheat oven to 375°F (190°C). Grease and flour two 8-inch, round pans. Combine BASIC CAKE MIX and milk in a large bowl. Beat at medium speed 2 minutes. Scrape bowl and beaters. Add egg whites and vanilla. Beat 2 more minutes. Pour into prepared pans. Bake 20 to 25 minutes, until a toothpick inserted in center comes out clean. Cool in pans 10 minutes, then cool on wire racks. Frost as desired. Makes one 2-layer cake, or 24 cupcakes.

Grandma's Picnic Cake

It's easy to carry along with you!

1 cup chopped dates
1 teaspoon baking soda
1½ cups boiling water
4 cups BASIC CAKE
   MIX, page 30
2 eggs, beaten

1 teaspoon cinnamon
1 teaspoon vanilla
¾ cup brown sugar,
   firmly packed
¾ cup chopped nuts
¾ cup chocolate chips

Preheat oven to 350°F (175°C). Grease a 13″ × 9″ baking pan. In a small bowl, combine dates, baking soda and boiling water. Set aside to cool. In a large bowl, combine BASIC CAKE MIX, eggs, cinnamon and vanilla. Beat at medium speed 2 to 3 minutes. Scrape bowl and beaters and beat 2 more minutes. Add date mixture. Beat 2 more minutes. Pour into prepared pan. Top with brown sugar, nuts and then chocolate chips. Bake 30 to 35 minutes, until a toothpick inserted in center comes out clean. Cool in pan 10 minutes, then cool on a wire rack. Makes 1 large cake.

Sugar & Spice Gingerbread

Make it the specialty of your house!

½ cup milk
1 egg
½ cup molasses
2¼ cups GINGER-
   BREAD MIX,
   page 31

Hot Lemon Sauce,
   see below
Whipped cream, or ice
   cream
Fresh sliced bananas or
   peaches

Hot Lemon Sauce:

1 cup water
¼ cup LEMON PIE-
   FILLING MIX,
   page 36

2 tablespoons butter or
   margarine

Preheat oven to 350°F (175°C). Butter and lightly flour a 9-inch square pan. Combine milk, egg and molasses in a medium bowl. Add GINGERBREAD MIX and stir until blended. Pour into prepared pan. Bake about 30 minutes, until a toothpick inserted in center comes out clean. Cool in pan 10 minutes, then cool on a wire rack. Serve with Hot Lemon Sauce and whipped cream or ice cream, or with fresh sliced bananas or peaches. Makes one 9-inch cake.

Hot Lemon Sauce:

Combine water and LEMON PIE-FILLING MIX in a small saucepan. Bring to a boil over high heat, stirring constantly. Remove from heat. Add butter or margarine and stir to melt. Serve warm over gingerbread, pound cake, apple pie or other desserts.

Sunny Yellow Cake

This is the traditional cake that
goes with many favorite frostings.

3⅓ cups BASIC CAKE MIX, page 30	1 teaspoon vanilla Orange Butter Cream Frosting, see below
¾ cup milk	
2 eggs, well beaten	

Orange Butter Cream Frosting:

⅓ cup soft butter or margarine	1½ tablespoons grated orange peel
3 cups sifted powdered sugar	3 tablespoons orange juice

Preheat oven to 375°F (190°C). Grease and lightly flour two 8-inch, round cake pans. In a large bowl, combine BASIC CAKE MIX and milk. Beat at medium speed 2 minutes. Scrape bowl and beaters. Add eggs and vanilla. Beat 2 more minutes, Pour into prepared pans. Bake 25 to 30 minutes, until a toothpick inserted in center comes out clean. Cool in pans 10 minutes, then cool on wire racks. Prepare Orange Butter Cream Frosting. Frost cooled cake. Makes one 2-layer cake.

Orange Butter Cream Frosting:

In a medium bowl, cream together butter or margarine and powdered sugar. Add grated orange peel and orange juice. Beat until smooth. Makes enough frosting for one cake.

Variation

To make orange cake, add 1 teaspoon grated orange peel to BASIC CAKE MIX. Substitute ½ teaspoon lemon extract for vanilla. Frost with Orange Butter Cream Frosting.

Pineapple Upside-Down Cake

A light, moist cake with a tangy fruit topping.

Brown Sugar Topping, see below	1 cup milk
3 cups QUICK MIX, page 30	3 eggs, slightly beaten
	1½ teaspoons vanilla
1⅓ cups sugar	1 (20-oz.) can crushed pineapple, drained

Brown Sugar Topping:

1 cup brown sugar, firmly packed	½ cup butter or margarine

Lightly butter a 13″ × 9″ baking pan or two 8-inch square pans. Prepare Brown Sugar Topping and set aside. Preheat oven to 350°F (175°C). Combine QUICK MIX and sugar in a large bowl. Mix well. In a small bowl, combine milk, eggs and vanilla. Add half of milk mixture to dry ingredients. Beat 2 minutes until batter is smooth. Add remaining milk mixture, and beat 2 to 3 more minutes. Pat Brown Sugar Topping evenly over bottom of pan. Spoon crushed pineapple smoothly over topping. Spread batter over pineapple.

Bake 45 to 50 minutes, until center springs back when lightly touched. Cool in pan 10 minutes, then invert onto a serving plate. Serve warm with pineapple side up. Makes one large cake or two 8-inch cakes.

Brown Sugar Topping:

In a small bowl, combine brown sugar and butter or margarine until mixture is evenly distributed.

Variation

Substitute thawed and drained, frozen or canned fruit for pineapple. Try peaches, apples, apricots, strawberries or raspberries. If using strawberries or raspberries, substitute granulated sugar for brown sugar.

How to Make Pineapple Upside-Down Cake

1/Pat the mixture of brown sugar and butter or margarine evenly over the bottom of two 8-inch pans or one 13" x 9" pan. Spoon crushed pineapple over mixture.

2/Use a rubber scraper to spread the batter mixture evenly over the Pineapple Topping.

3/Cool the cake 10 minutes in the pan, then invert onto a serving plate. Serve it warm, upside-down.

Southern Pound Cake

*Show your Southern hospitality by
serving this to your friends.*

3½ cups BASIC CAKE
    MIX, page 30
1 (4-oz.) pkg. instant
    vanilla pudding
½ cup vegetable oil
1 cup milk

4 eggs
1 teaspoon vanilla
Hot Lemon Sauce, pages
    200–201, or powdered
    sugar, if desired

Preheat oven to 375°F (190°C). Generously grease
and lightly flour a bundt pan. In a large bowl, combine BASIC CAKE MIX, instant vanilla pudding, oil
and milk. Beat at medium speed 4 minutes. Scrape
bowl and beaters. Add eggs 1 at a time, beating well
after each. Pour into prepared pan. Bake 40 to 45
minutes, until a toothpick inserted in center comes out
clean. Cool in pan 10 minutes, then cool on a wire
rack. Serve with Hot Lemon Sauce or sprinkle with
powdered sugar, if desired. Makes 1 bundt cake.

Lazy Daisy Cake

It's as delicious as it is quick.

3 cups QUICK MIX,
    page 15
1⅓ cups sugar
1 cup milk

3 eggs, slightly beaten
1½ teaspoons vanilla
Lazy Daisy Topping,
    see below

Lazy Daisy Topping:

¾ cup brown sugar,
    firmly packed
6 tablespoons butter or
    margarine

1⅓ cups coconut
⅓ cup milk

Preheat oven to 350°F (175°C). Grease and flour a
13″ × 9″ baking pan. Combine QUICK MIX and

sugar in a large bowl. Mix well. In a small bowl, combine milk, eggs and vanilla. Add half of milk mixture to dry ingredients. Beat 2 to 3 minutes, until batter is smooth. Add remaining milk mixture and beat 3 more minutes. Pour into prepared pan and spread evenly. Bake 35 to 40 minutes, until a toothpick inserted in center comes out clean. Immediately spread with Lazy Daisy Topping. Return cake to oven and broil 3 to 4 minutes, until topping becomes bubbly and light brown. Serve warm. Makes 1 large cake.

Lazy Daisy Topping:

In a small bowl, mix together brown sugar and butter or margarine until blended. Add coconut and milk. Makes enough topping for one large cake.

Variation

Nutty Pineapple-Coconut Topping: Omit Lazy Daisy Topping. Combine 1 cup firmly packed brown sugar and 6 tablespoons butter or margarine in a small bowl. Add 1 cup coconut, ⅔ cup drained crushed pineapple and ½ cup chopped nuts. Mix well. Makes enough topping for one large cake.

Rich Spice Cake

*If you're a raisin fan, add a
handful of raisins to the batter.*

3⅓ cups BASIC CAKE
   MIX, page 30
1 teaspoon nutmeg
1 teaspoon cinnamon
½ teaspoon cloves
1 cup water
¼ cup butter or
   margarine
1 cup brown sugar,
   firmly packed

½ cup sour cream
2 eggs
½ cup chopped nuts
Raisins, if desired
Caramel Icing, see below
¼ cup chopped nuts,
   if desired

Caramel Icing:

½ cup butter or
  margarine
½ cup brown sugar,
  firmly packed

⅓ cup milk
2¼ cups powdered sugar
1 teaspoon vanilla

Preheat oven to 375°F (190°C). Generously grease a
15″ × 10″ baking pan. In a large bowl, combine
BASIC CAKE MIX, nutmeg, cinnamon and cloves. In
a small saucepan, combine water, butter or margarine
and brown sugar. Bring to a boil. Add to dry ingredients. Mix well. Add sour cream, eggs, ½ cup chopped
nuts and raisins, if desired. Pour into prepared pan.
Bake 20 to 25 minutes, until a toothpick inserted in center comes out clean. Cool cake in pan. Prepare Caramel
Icing. Frost cooled cake. Top with chopped nuts, if
desired. Makes 1 large cake.

Caramel Icing:

Melt butter or margarine over low heat in a small
saucepan. Add brown sugar and boil over low heat 2
minutes, stirring constantly. Add milk and bring to a
boil. Cool to lukewarm. Put powdered sugar in a
medium bowl. Add butter mixture and vanilla. Beat
with an electric mixer until smooth.

Texas Sheet Cake

A B-i-i-i-g Brownie Cake!

4 cups BROWNIE MIX,
   page 36
½ cup butter or
   margarine
1 cup water

½ cup sour cream
2 eggs, slightly beaten
1 teaspoon baking soda
Cocoa Icing, see below

Cocoa Icing:

3 cups powdered sugar
½ cup evaporated milk
½ cup butter or
   margarine

3 tablespoons cocoa
1 cup chopped nuts
1 teaspoon vanilla

Preheat oven to 375°F (190°C). Grease a 15″ × 10″ or larger baking pan. Put BROWNIE MIX in a large bowl. In a small saucepan, bring butter or margarine and water to a boil. Add to BROWNIE MIX. Add sour cream, eggs and baking soda. Blend well. Pour into prepared pan. Bake 20 to 25 minutes, until a toothpick inserted in center comes out clean. Prepare Cocoa Icing. Frost cake while still hot. Makes one large cake.

Cocoa Icing:

In a small saucepan, being evaporated milk, butter or margarine and cocoa to a boil, stirring constantly. Remove from heat. Add to powdered sugar in a medium bowl. Stir in nuts and vanilla.

To make milk sour, add 1 teaspoon vinegar to ½ cup milk.

MORE DESSERTS

Children might have the right idea when they eat main dishes sparingly to save room for the finishing touch—dessert! A meal without a dessert is like a kitchen without a sink. Many desserts add nutrition to a meal, such as puddings and fruit-filled pies and desserts.

When planning your menus, include desserts that will complement the meal. For example, serve a light dessert such as Lemonade Ice Cream Pie when having a meal of pasta or other substantial food. Save your rich desserts like Banana Split Cake or Blueberry Dessert for lighter meals. All-American Apple Pie is good served at any time with any meal. It's even more appealing with rich Hot Butter Sauce. MOIST PIE CRUST MIX, page 40, is great for any pie.

The COOKIE CRUMB CRUST MIX, page 37–38, can be used in all recipes that call for a graham cracker crust or baked crust. Simply press the amount of COOKIE CRUMB CRUST MIX you desire, about 2 cups per 8-inch square pan, into the bottom of the pan, and proceed with the recipe. CRUMB TOPPING MIX makes a great topper for fruit desserts, puddings and ice cream.

This section includes family desserts for everyday, such as Mississippi Mud, Apple-Walnut Cobbler and Impossible Pie, which forms its own crust. For special occasions we have included Brownie Alaska and Layered Raspberry Cheesecake. Cream Puffs Supreme are so easy you'll find yourself making them often. All of these desserts are delectable enough to win a bouquet of compliments.

209

All-American Apple Pie

It's exquisite!

1 Moist Pie Crust, page
    40, or Flaky Pie Crust,
    page 39
7 or 8 tart cooking
    apples, pared, cored
    and sliced thin
Juice of 1 lemon
    (about ¼ cup)

6 tablespoons flour
¾ cup sugar, more if
    desired
1 teaspoon cinnamon
1 teaspoon nutmeg
2 tablespoons butter

Hot Butter Sauce:

½ cup butter
1 cup sugar
1 cup cream, or
    evaporated milk

Dash of nutmeg

Prepare pie crust. Put apples in a large bowl. Toss with lemon juice. Set aside. Preheat oven to 400°F (205°C). In a small bowl, combine flour, sugar, cinnamon and nutmeg. Sprinkle about ¼ cup of mixture on the pie crust and add the rest to the apples. Stir to coat apples. Fill pie crust heaping full of apple mixture. Dot with butter. Place top crust over filling. Press edges together and flute. Cut slits in top crust. Bake about 50 minutes, until crust is golden. Serve with Hot Butter Sauce. Makes one 9-inch double-crust pie.

Hot Butter Sauce:

Combine butter, sugar and cream or evaporated milk in a small saucepan. Cook over medium heat about 3 to 5 minutes, until butter melts and sugar is dissolved. Do not boil. Remove from heat. Add nutmeg. Serve warm. Makes about 1¼ cups sauce.

Luscious Lemon Pie

Tart and well worth the pucker!

1 baked Flaky Pie Crust,
    page 39, or Moist Pie
    Crust, page 40
1¼ cups LEMON PIE-
    FILLING MIX,
    page 36

2½ cups water
3 egg yolks
2 tablespoons butter or
    margarine
Sweetened whipped
    cream

Prepare pie crust. In a large saucepan, combine LEMON PIE-FILLING MIX, ½ cup of the water and egg yolks. Mix until smooth. Add remaining 2 cups water. Cook over medium heat, about 4 to 5 minutes, stirring constantly, until mixture is thick and bubbly. Remove from heat. Add butter or margarine. Stir until melted. Cover and let cool 5 minutes. Stir. Pour into baked pie crust. Cover and refrigerate 3 hours. Top with whipped cream before serving. Makes one 9-inch single-crust pie.

Variation

Meringue Topping: Omit whipped cream topping. In a deep metal or glass bowl, beat 3 egg whites until stiff, gradually adding 6 tablespoons sugar. Spread on top of warm pie, sealing to edges. Preheat oven to 400°F (205°C). Bake 8 to 10 minutes, until meringue is lightly browned. Cool pie on a wire rack, then refrigerate.

Vanilla Cream Pie

*Master this technique and you'll have
many delightful desserts at your fingertips.*

1 baked Flaky Pie Crust,
   page 39, or Moist Pie
   Crust, page 40
1¼ cups PUDDING &
   PIE MIX, page 37
2¾ cups milk

2 eggs, well-beaten
1 teaspoon vanilla
2 tablespoons butter or
   margarine
Whipped cream

Prepare pie crust. Combine PUDDING & PIE MIX
and 1 cup of the milk in a heavy saucepan. Stir until
smooth. Gradually add remaining 1¾ cups milk. Cook
over medium heat about 5 to 7 minutes, stirring constantly, until mixture comes to a boil and thickens. Remove from heat. Gradually add half of hot mixture to
beaten eggs in a medium bowl. Mix well. Blend egg
mixture slowly into the remaining hot mixture in saucepan. Cook about 1 minute, stirring constantly, until
mixture just begins to boil. Remove from heat. Stir in
vanilla and butter or margarine. Cool, then pour into
pie crust. Refrigerate 2 to 3 hours, until firm. Serve
with whipped cream. Makes one 9-inch single-crust pie.

Variations

Coconut Cream Pie: Add 1 cup flaked coconut to filling before pouring into pie crust.
Banana Cream Pie: Slice 2 bananas into pie crust before pouring in filling.
Blueberry Cream Pie. Top cooled pie with 1 can blueberry pie filling.
Vanilla Pudding: Increase milk to 3 cups.

Chocolate Cream Pie

Smooth!

1 baked Flaky Pie Crust,
    page 39, or Moist Pie
    Crust, page 40
1¼ cups PUDDING &
    PIE MIX, page 37
¼ cup sugar
¼ cup cocoa

2¾ cups milk
2 eggs, well-beaten
1 teaspoon vanilla
3 tablespoons butter or
    margarine
Whipped cream

Prepare pie crust. In a small bowl, combine PUD-
DING & PIE MIX, sugar and cocoa until well-blended.
In a heavy saucepan, combine cocoa mixture and 1
cup of the milk. Stir until smooth. Gradually add remaining 1¾ cups milk and cook over medium heat
about 5 to 7 minutes, stirring constantly, until mixture
boils and thickens. Remove from heat. Gradually add
half of hot mixture to the beaten eggs in a medium
bowl. Mix well. Blend egg mixture slowly into the remaining hot mixture in saucepan. Cook about 1 minute, stirring constantly, until mixture just begins to boil.
Remove from heat. Stir in vanilla and butter or margarine. Cool, then pour into pie crust. Refrigerate 2 to 3
hours, until firm. Serve with whipped cream. Makes
one 9-inch single-crust pie.

Variation

Chocolate Pudding: Increase milk to 3 cups.

Turnover Fried Pies

Main dish or dessert.
You choose by the filling you use.

Vegetable oil for frying
2 cups QUICK MIX,
    page 15

½ cup milk or water
Fruit Filling, see below

Preheat 1 inch of oil to 350°F (175°C) in an electric skillet. Combine QUICK MIX and milk or water in a medium bowl. Stir to blend. On a lightly floured surface, knead about 15 times, until dough is smooth. Roll dough as for pie crust. Cut into 5-inch-diameter circles. Place 1 to 2 tablespoons of filling on half of each circle. Fold dough over and press the edges firmly with fork tines dipped in flour. Fry in hot oil about 2 minutes on each side, until golden brown. Makes 8 to 10 turnover pies.

Fruit Fillings

Applesauce: Fill with thick, flavored applesauce.
Fresh Fruit: Fill with fresh, cut-up, sweetened fruit such as strawberries, peaches, apricots or raspberries.
Canned Pie Fillings: Fill with any fruit pie filling such as cherry, blueberry and lemon.
Dried Fruit: Fill with cooked dried apricots, peaches or apples with 3 tablespoons sugar added to fruit mixture.
Pineapple: Fill with mixture of ⅔ cup drained crushed pineapple, 4 teaspoons sugar and 2 teaspoons cornstarch, cooked together until thickened, then cooled.
Mincemeat: Fill with mixture of equal parts mincemeat and thick applesauce.

Main Dish Fillings

Chili: Fill with thick homemade or canned chili.
Chicken or Tuna: Fill with mixture of 1 cup minced, cooked chicken or tuna, 1 tablespoon chopped pimiento or parsley and ¼ cup chicken gravy or cream of chicken soup.
Runza: Fill with mixture of ¼ cup minced onion and ¼ pound lean ground beef, browned together and combined with 1 cup shredded cabbage, ½ teaspoon salt and pepper to taste. Cook together 5 minutes and drain before filling pies.

Impossible Pie

*This pie forms its own custard on the
bottom with a cake-like crust on top.*

½ cup sugar
4 eggs
2 cups milk
1 teaspoon vanilla
3 tablespoons butter or
  margarine, melted

½ teaspoon cinnamon
¼ teaspoon nutmeg
½ cup QUICK MIX,
  page 15

Preheat oven to 400°F (205°C). Butter a 9-inch pie
plate. In a blender, combine sugar, eggs, milk, vanilla,
melted butter or margarine, cinnamon and nutmeg.
Blend until smooth. Add QUICK MIX and blend
30 more seconds. Pour into prepared pie pan. Bake 25
to 30 minutes, until golden. Cool on a wire rack. Serve
warm. Makes one 9-inch pie.

Cream Puffs Supreme

Try party-size cream puffs for appetizers!

1½ cups water
2 cups QUICK MIX,
  page 15
4 eggs

Filling, as desired
Fudge Sauce, see below,
  or powdered sugar

Fudge Sauce:

1 cup BROWNIE MIX,
  page 36
½ cup water, more if
  desired

½ cup chopped nuts,
  if desired

Preheat oven to 450°F (230°C). Lightly grease baking
sheets. Bring water to a boil in a medium saucepan.
Add QUICK MIX. Stir over low heat about 5 minutes,
until dough forms a smooth ball. Remove from heat

immediately. Add eggs 1 at a time, blending after each. Beat vigorously. Drop by large tablespoonfuls onto baking sheets. Bake about 15 minutes. Reduce heat to 350°F (175°C), and bake 20 more minutes, until golden brown. Let stand in warm oven with door open about 10 minutes to dry out. Cool on wire racks. Freeze for later use, if desired. To fill, cut off top third of cream puffs. Remove any remaining dough in centers and fill as desired. Replace tops. Frost with Fudge Sauce or sprinkle with powdered sugar. Keep refrigerated until serving time. Makes about 10 large cream puffs.

Fudge Sauce:

In a small saucepan, blend BROWNIE MIX and water. Cook over medium heat about 3 minutes, stirring constantly, until mixture comes to a boil. Reduce heat. Cover and simmer about 1 minute, until sauce is thick and smooth. Add nuts, if desired. Use as topping for brownies, or filling for cake, or served hot over vanilla ice cream. Makes 1 cup sauce.

Variations

Appetizer Cream Puffs: Drop dough by large teaspoonfuls onto baking sheets. Bake 10 minutes at 450°F (230°C), then 15 minutes at 350°F (175°C). Makes 25 to 30 small cream puffs.

Vanilla Cream Puffs: Make Vanilla Cream Pie filling, page 212, or prepare 1 (3-oz.) package vanilla pudding mix according to package directions. Cool. In a medium bowl, whip 1 cup whipping cream. Fold into pudding mixture. Fill cream puffs.

Hot Fudge Cream Puff Sundaes: Fill each cream puff with about ½ cup vanilla ice cream. Top with scoop of Fudge Sauce. Garnish with chopped nuts, cherries and whipped cream, as desired.

Hot Chicken Salad Boats: See Hot Chicken Salad, page 160.

Seafood Rice Puffs: See pages 161–162

Peach Blossom Dessert

Peaches and oatmeal—WOW!

2½ cups OATMEAL
MIX, page 15
½ cup brown sugar,
firmly packed

1 (21-oz.) can peach pie
filling
Ice cream or whipped
cream, if desired

Preheat oven to 375°F (190°C). Lightly grease an 8-inch square pan. Combine OATMEAL MIX and brown sugar in a medium bowl. Press half of mixture into prepared pan. Pour peach pie filling over top. Crumble remaining half of oatmeal mixture over the peach filling. Bake 30 minutes, until lightly browned. Cut in large squares. Serve warm with ice cream or whipped cream. Makes 8 to 10 servings.

Variation

Substitute French apple pie filling for peach pie filling.

Apple-Walnut Cobbler

Create a cobbler with your favorite fruit!
Try it with CRUMB TOPPING MIX, page 226.

4 cups peeled, cored and
sliced apples
½ cup sugar
½ teaspoon cinnamon
¾ cup coarsely chopped
walnuts

2 cups QUICK MIX,
page 15
3 tablespoons sugar
1 egg, slightly beaten
1 cup milk or water
Whipped cream

Preheat oven to 325°F (165°C). Lightly grease an 8-inch square pan. Place apples in bottom of pan. Combine sugar, cinnamon and walnuts in a small bowl. Sprinkle over apples in pan, reserving ¼ cup for topping. In a medium bowl, combine QUICK MIX and sugar until well-blended. Combine egg and milk or water in a small bowl. Add all at once to dry ingredients. Blend. Spread dough evenly over top of apple mixture. Top with remaining cinnamon-sugar mixture. Bake about 45 minutes, until light brown. Cut into squares and serve with whipped cream. Makes about 8 to 10 servings.

Variation

Cherry Cobbler: Omit apples, sugar, cinnamon and walnuts. Drain and reserve liquid from 1 (16-oz.) can red, sour, pitted cherries. Combine 2 tablespoons flour, ¾ cup sugar and ⅛ teaspoon salt. Gradually stir in reserved cherry juice. Blend until smooth. Fold in cherries and 1 teaspoon almond extract. Make cobbler mixture, reducing milk or water to 6 tablespoons and adding 1 teaspoon almond extract. Bake at 425°F (220°C) about 25 minutes.

Banana Split Cake

And you thought banana splits were made from ice cream!

2 cups COOKIE CRUMB CRUST MIX, pages 37–38
¼ cup butter or margarine, melted
2 eggs
1 cup butter or margarine, softened
2 cups sifted powdered sugar
3 to 4 bananas

1 (15¼-oz.) can crushed pineapple, drained
1 (13½-oz.) carton whipped topping, thawed, or 1 pint sweetened whipped cream
¼ to ½ cup chopped nuts

In a medium bowl, combine COOKIE CRUMB CRUST MIX and ¼ cup melted butter or margarine. Press into an unbuttered 13″ × 9″ pan. In a medium bowl, combine eggs, 1 cup butter or margarine and powdered sugar. Beat 10 to 15 minutes, until smooth.

Spread over crust in pan. Slice bananas evenly over top of mixture. Spread crushed pineapple evenly over bananas. Top with whipped topping or whipped cream. Sprinkle with nuts. Refrigerate 3 to 4 hours. Makes about 12 servings.

How to Make Banana Split Cake

1/Press COOKIE CRUMB CRUST MIX into an unbuttered baking dish. Spread the mixture of eggs, butter or margarine and powdered sugar over the crust.

2/Slice bananas evenly over the mixture and spoon drained, crushed pineapple over the bananas.

3/Top the cake with whipped topping, sprinkle with nuts and refrigerate. Don't bake this dessert!

Lemonade Ice Cream Dessert

A light and cool dessert to top off any meal.

3 cups COOKIE
CRUMB CRUST
MIX, pages 37–38
½ gallon vanilla ice
cream, softened

1 (6-oz.) can frozen
lemonade concentrate

Press 2 cups of the COOKIE CRUMB CRUST MIX
into an 11″ × 7″ baking pan. Put softened ice cream
and frozen lemonade concentrate in a large bowl. Beat
with an electric mixer until well-blended. Quickly
spoon ice cream mixture into crumb-lined pan. Top
with remaining 1 cup crumbs. Freeze. Slice and serve.
Makes 15 to 20 servings.

---

*For a glossy brown crust on fruit pies, lightly
brush the top crust with milk before baking and
sprinkle it lightly with sugar.*

Brownie Alaska

*Prepare it ahead of time for
a spectacular, but simple dessert.*

1 quart vanilla ice cream,
  softened slightly
2 cups BROWNIE MIX,
  page 36
4 eggs, separated

2 tablespoons water
1 teaspoon vanilla
½ cup coarsely chopped
  walnuts
½ cup sugar

Line a medium bowl with aluminum foil. Pack ice
cream into bowl and freeze until very firm. Preheat
oven to 350°F (175°C). Grease an 8-inch, round cake
pan. Line pan with wax paper. Grease wax paper. In
another medium bowl, combine BROWNIE MIX, egg
yolks, water, vanilla and nuts. Spread in prepared pan.
Bake about 25 minutes, until edges separate from pan.
Cool in pan 10 minutes, then cool on a wire rack.
Carefully peel off wax paper. Place cake in the center
of a wooden cutting board or a baking sheet lined with
heavy brown paper. Cover with plastic wrap. Chill in
freezer about 1 hour until hard. In a glass or metal
bowl, beat egg whites until foamy. Gradually add sugar
and beat until stiff peaks form. Set aside. Quickly invert bowl of ice cream over cake. Lift off bowl and remove foil. Quickly spread meringue evenly over ice
cream and brownie, sealing meringue to cutting board
or paper. Return to freezer at least 30 minutes. Just
before serving, preheat oven to 500°F (260°C). Bake
about 3 minutes, until meringue is lightly browned. Cut
in wedges with a knife dipped in warm water. Refreeze
leftover Brownie Alaska, if desired. Makes 10 to 12
servings.

Variation

Substitute mint chocolate chip or peppermint ice cream
for vanilla ice cream.

Sunday Shortcake

The old-fashioned way, with your choice of fruit.

3 cups QUICK MIX,
  page 15
2 tablespoons sugar
¼ cup butter or
  margarine, melted

½ cup milk or water
1 egg, well-beaten
Fruit, as desired
Whipped cream

Preheat oven to 400°F (205°C). Combine QUICK MIX and sugar in a medium bowl. Mix well. In a small bowl, combine melted butter or margarine, milk or water and egg. Add to dry ingredients. Stir with a fork until just moistened. On a lightly floured surface, knead 8 to 10 times. Roll out dough to ½-inch thickness. Cut with a lightly floured 3-inch, round cutter. Bake on an unbuttered baking sheet about 10 minutes, until golden brown. Cool. Top with fruit as desired and whipped cream. Makes 6 shortcakes.

Mississippi Mud

Appropriately named for its appearance—and incredibly delicious!

4 eggs
½ cup butter or
  margarine, melted
3 cups BROWNIE MIX,
  page 36
1 teaspoon vanilla

2 cups chopped nuts
1 cup flaked coconut
1 (7-oz.) jar marsh-
  mallow creme
Chocolate Icing, see
  below

Chocolate Icing:

1 lb. powdered sugar
½ cup butter or margarine
6 tablespoons evaporated
  milk

4 tablespoons cocoa

Preheat oven to 350°F (175°C). Lightly grease and lightly flour a 13″ × 9″ baking pan. In a large bowl, beat eggs until foamy. Add melted butter or margarine and mix well. Add BROWNIE MIX and blend well. Stir in vanilla. Stir in nuts and coconut. Pour into prepared pan. Bake about 30 minutes, until edges separate from pan. While still hot, carefully spread on marshmallow creme. Frost with Chocolate Icing. Makes 1 large cake.

Chocolate Icing:

Put powdered sugar in a medium bowl. In a small saucepan, combine butter or margarine, evaporated milk and cocoa. Bring to a boil, stirring constantly. Remove from heat. Immediately add to powdered sugar. Beat until smooth.

Layered Raspberry Cheesecake

A Danish delight!

1½ cups COOKIE
CRUMB CRUST
MIX, pages 37–38
1 envelope whipped
topping mix
½ cup cold milk
½ teaspoon vanilla
1 (3-oz.) pkg. cream
cheese, softened

½ cup sifted powdered
sugar
1 (4¾-oz.) pkg.
raspberry-currant
Danish Dessert®
1¾ cups water
1 (10-oz.) pkg. frozen
raspberries, thawed
and drained

Press COOKIE CRUMB CRUST MIX into a 9-inch pie plate. In a medium bowl, prepare whipped topping mix with cold milk and vanilla according to package directions. Add softened cream cheese and powdered sugar. Blend well. Spread evenly over crust. Refrigerate about 1 hour. In a medium saucepan, combine Danish Dessert® with water or drained raspberry juice and cook according to package directions. Cool. Add raspberries. Pour mixture evenly over cream cheese mixture. Cover and refrigerate. Makes about 8 servings.

Blueberry Dessert

A delightfully different party dessert.

3 cups COOKIE CRUMB
    CRUST MIX, pages
    37–38
2 eggs
1 cup butter or
    margarine
2 cups powdered sugar
2 (3-oz.) pkgs. cream
    cheese

1 (21-oz.) can blue-
    berry pie filling
1 cup whipping cream,
    whipped
½ cup chopped pecans

Press all but 2 tablespoons COOKIE CRUMB CRUST
MIX onto the bottom of an 11″ × 7″ baking pan. In
a medium bowl, cream together eggs, butter or margarine, powdered sugar and cream cheese until smooth.
Spread over crumb layer. Spread blueberry pie filling
evenly over top. Top with whipped cream and sprinkle with a mixture of remaining 2 tablespoons crumbs
and pecans. Refrigerate at least 12 hours. Cut into
squares. Makes 15 to 20 servings.

Crumb Topping Mix

This topping is tops!

1⅓ cups brown sugar,
   firmly packed
1 cup all-purpose flour
2 teaspoons cinnamon

½ teaspoon nutmeg
¾ cup butter or
   margarine

In a medium bowl, combine brown sugar, flour and cinnamon. Mix well. With a pastry blender, cut in butter or margarine until mixture is very fine. Put in a 1-quart, airtight container. Label. Store in the refrigerator. Use within 1 to 2 months. Makes about 2 cups of CRUMB TOPPING MIX.

CRUMB TOPPING MIX makes:

Topping on cobblers,
   fruit pies, puddings,
   ice cream and
   fruit cups.

Let's Go Camping

Mixes are the way to go gourmet when you go camping. On any trip or outing, they make for hearty eating with instant cooking. Mixes are suited for backpacking because they are lightweight and compact. GRANOLA MIX is a great snack for hikers.

You may find it more convenient to prepare certain foods from mixes before you leave home, such as cookies, rolls and cakes. But for pancakes, biscuits, Indian Fry Bread and other recipes, just premeasure the amount of mix you need in sealed heavy plastic bags. Label the mix and list the ingredients to be added. When it is time to make your meal, just add the liquid ingredients, close the bag securely and blend the ingredients by gently squeezing the bag about 30 to 40 seconds. That means no fuss, no mess and no dishes to wash! It won't be hard to get volunteers to do this type of mixing.

Take some frozen meat mixes with you! Your meat supply will keep fresh longer, while the frozen containers keep the other foods in your ice chest cold. Just cook the mixes in a skillet or saucepan until heated through. Again, the preparation and cleanup are minimal.

Take a trip with mixes this weekend, and they'll become a "must" for future adventures.

For a 3-day menu we suggest:

First Day

Breakfast
Favorite Wheat Pancakes, page 91, (WHEAT MIX)
Bacon & Eggs
Orange Juice

Lunch
Rancher's Sloppy Joes, page 125, (MEAT SAUCE MIX)
Carrot Sticks & Celery Sticks

Potato Chips
Russian Refresher, page 45, (RUSSIAN REFRESHER MIX)
Molasses Cookies, page 178, (QUICK MIX)

Snack
Apples

Supper
Saturday Stroganoff, page 148, (READY HAM-BURGER MIX)
Canned Vegetables
Karine's Drop Biscuits, page 105, (QUICK MIX)
Lemonade
Our Best Brownies, page 184, (BROWNIE MIX)

Second Day

Breakfast
Granola, pages 33–34, (GRANOLA MIX)
Fresh Fruit
Hot Chocolate, page 46, (HOT CHOCOLATE MIX)

Lunch
Indian Fry Bread, page 97, (QUICK MIX), served with beans, topped with cheese, tomatoes and lettuce
Orange Drink
Sugar Cookies, page 170, (QUICK MIX)

Snack
Cinnamon Rolls, page 73, (HOT ROLL MIX)

Supper
Grilled Hamburger Patties or Steaks
Baked Potatoes, cooked in coals
Corn on the cob, cooked in coals
Coleslaw
Russian Refresher, page 45, (RUSSIAN REFRESHER MIX)
Cherry Dessert Cake, page 197, (BASIC CAKE MIX)

Third Day

Breakfast
Nevada's Pancakes, page 92, (QUICK MIX)
Sausage & Eggs
Orange Juice
Hot Chocolate, page 46, (HOT CHOCOLATE MIX)

Lunch
Chicken Burgers, page 132, (CHICKEN MIX)
Corn chips
Marinated Bean Salad
Lemonade
Cinnamon Thins, page 179, (QUICK MIX)

Snack
Banana

Supper
Chili, page 61, (CHILI SEASONING MIX)
Cheese & Crackers
Milk
Grandma's Picnic Cake, page 200, (BASIC CAKE
MIX)

Let's Make Gifts

Tired of racking your brain for an idea every time you need a gift for a special occasion? With Master Mixes and Special Mixes you have a multitude of creative gifts at your fingertips. Mixes keep for months, so the recipients will enjoy your gifts fully.

You'll want to include Make-A-Mix Cookery recipes with your mixes! See pages 233 to 244 for a collection of gift tags with recipes to attach to your gifts. Punch a hole in them and fasten them with a ribbon or tape them to your gift package.

Package your mixes in decorative containers that can be used in the preparation of the mix or for serving purposes. As a bonus, give a sample of products that can be made with the mix!

Begin your mix with these ideas:

Meal-in-Minutes: Give a complete meal of mixes! Fill a picnic basket with SPAGHETTI SEASONING MIX, page 62, HOT ROLL MIX, page 17, CAESAR SALAD DRESSING MIX, page 52, and BASIC COOKIE MIX, page 32.

Joys of Gingerbread: Decorate Gingerbread Boys, page 168, with sugar-coated chocolate candies. Include a container of GINGERBREAD MIX, page 31. Pack it in a festive basket, topped with a pretty bow.

Tea Time: Pack some small bags of RUSSIAN REFRESHER MIX, page 45, in a small tea kettle. Attach a mint sprig and a ribbon.

Cups of Cocoa: Give HOT CHOCOLATE MIX, page 45, in a large mug or a set of mugs.

Family Favorite: Send some young folks a cookie jar filled with BASIC COOKIE MIX, page 32. Tie a cookie cutter to the top and deliver it with a batch of cookies. Include recipes!

Birthday Bakery: Bake a birthday cake from BASIC CAKE MIX, page 30, and wrap up a container of mix so they can enjoy more later.

Teenage Treat: Give a favorite babysitter or teen-ager a wooden canister filled with Big Soft Pretzels, pages 102–104. Or varnish pretzels and glue them on a wood plaque for a decorator item. Give HOT ROLL MIX, page 17, with either.

Brownies on Board: Arrange Our Best Brownies, page 184, on a cutting board with a container of BROWNIE MIX, page 36. Wrap with plastic wrap.

Crock & Cornbread: Anyone will be thrilled to receive CORNMEAL MIX, pages 17–18, and a crock of Honey Butter, page 100. Decorate the crock with a honey dipper with a small decorative honeybee attached.

Pancake Paradise: PANCAKE MIX, page 19, makes a nice gift with jars of fancy fruit-flavored syrups or jams.

Camper's Combination: Your outdoor friends would love WHEAT MIX, page 20, or GRANOLA MIX, pages 33–34. Package the mixes in a "mess" kit, canteen or a potato chip canister that can be used for storing camping utensils.

Italian Idea: Fill a tall, clear canister or apothecary jar with spaghetti. Give it with a container of frozen ITALIAN MEAT SAUCE MIX, pages 26–27, and the recipe for making a real Italian dinner.

Mexican Mixer: A package of taco shells could be included with several packages of TACO SEASON-ING MIX, page 64.

Garden Grown: Wrap a package of garden seeds with frozen GARDEN VEGETABLE MIX, page 29, and recipes for soups and main dishes.

Spice Specialties: What a delightful gift it would be to receive a spice rack full of Seasoning Mixes, pages 58 and 64. For a decorative wall hanging, put a variety of Seasoning Mixes in foil packets. Wrap the mixes inside circles of calico print fabric and tie them with yarn. Attach the packets to a strip of braided yarn and hang from a wooden ring.

Savory Salad: A salad dressing cruet would look nice with several packets of Salad Dressing Mixes, pages 51 to 57, inside.

Quick Cookery: QUICK MIX, page 15, makes so many great recipes, give everyone their own copy of MAKE-A-MIX COOKERY to go with it!

HOT
CHOCOLATE MIX
from
MAKE-A-MIX COOKERY
by Eliason, Harward & Westover
Published by Bantam
MIXED FOR YOU BY:

To Make 1 serving of Hot Chocolate:
Add 3 tablespoons of HOT CHOCOLATE
MIX to 1 cup hot water.
Stir to dissolve.

HOT ROLL MIX
from
MAKE-A-MIX COOKERY
by Eliason, Harward & Westover
Published by Bantam
MIXED FOR YOU BY:

HOT ROLL MIX makes:
Crescent Rolls

HOT CHOCOLATE MIX

1 (25.6-oz.) pkg. instant nonfat dry milk (10-2/3 cups)
1 (6-oz.) jar imitation powdered cream
2 cups powdered sugar
1 (16-oz.) can instant chocolate drink mix

Combine all ingredients in a large bowl. Mix well. Put
in a large airtight container. Label. Store in a cool, dry
place. Use within 6 months. Makes about 17 cups of
HOT CHOCOLATE MIX, enough for about 100 cups
of Hot Chocolate.

CRESCENT ROLLS

In a large bowl, dissolve 1 tablespoon active dry yeast
in 1-1/2 cups lukewarm water. Blend in 2 beaten eggs
and 1/2 cup vegetable oil or melted margarine. Add 5
cups HOT ROLL MIX. Blend well. Add additional HOT
ROLL MIX to make a soft, but not too sticky dough.
Knead about 5 minutes until dough is smooth. Lightly
butter bowl. Put dough in bowl and turn to butter top.
Cover dough with a damp towel and let rise in a warm
place until doubled in bulk, about 1 hour. Generously
grease baking sheets. Punch down dough. Divide in half.
Let stand 10 minutes. On a lightly floured surface, roll
out each half to a 12-inch circle. Brush each circle with
1 tablespoon soft butter or margarine. Cut each circle
into 16 pie-shaped wedges. Roll up each wedge from the
wide end. Place point-side down in a crescent shape on
prepared baking sheets. Cover and let rise again until
doubled in bulk, about 45 to 60 minutes. Preheat oven
to 400°F (205°C). Bake 15 to 20 minutes, until golden
brown. Makes about 32 rolls.

BROWNIE MIX
from
MAKE-A-MIX COOKERY
by Eliason, Harward & Westover
Published by Bantam
MIXED FOR YOU BY:

BROWNIE MIX makes:
Chewy Chocolate Cookies
Our Best Brownies

RUSSIAN
REFRESHER MIX
from
MAKE-A-MIX COOKERY
by Eliason, Harward & Westover
Published by Bantam
MIXED FOR YOU BY:

To make 1 serving of Russian Refresher:
Add 2 to 3 teaspoons RUSSIAN
REFRESHER MIX to 1 cup hot water.
Stir to dissolve.

CHEWY
CHOCOLATE COOKIES

Preheat oven to 375°F (190°C). Grease baking sheets.
Combine 2 eggs and 1/4 cup water in a medium bowl.
Beat with a fork until blended. Stir in 2-1/4 cups
BROWNIE MIX, 1/2 teaspoon baking soda, 3/4 cup
flour and 1 teaspoon vanilla. Blend well. Drop by tea-
spoonfuls 2 inches apart onto prepared baking sheets.
Put a walnut or pecan half in center of each cookie.
Bake 10 to 12 minutes, until edges are browned. Cool
on wire racks. Makes about 3 dozen cookies.

OUR BEST BROWNIES

Preheat oven to 350°F (175°C). Grease and flour an
8-inch square pan. In a medium bowl, combine 2 beaten
eggs, 1 teaspoon vanilla and 2-1/2 cups BROWNIE
MIX. Beat until smooth. Stir in 1/2 cup chopped nuts.
Pour into prepared pan. Bake 30 to 35 minutes, until
edges separate from pan. Cool. Cut into 2-inch bars.
Sprinkle with powdered sugar or your choice of topping.
Makes 16 brownies.

RUSSIAN
REFRESHER MIX

2 cups powdered orange drink mix
1 (3-oz.) pkg. presweetened powdered lemonade mix
1-1/3 cups sugar
1 teaspoon cinnamon
1/2 teaspoon ground cloves

Combine all ingredients in a medium bowl. Mix well.
Put in a 1-quart airtight container. Label. Store in a
cool, dry place. Use within 6 months. Makes about
3-1/2 cups of RUSSIAN REFRESHER MIX, enough
for about 55 cups Russian Refresher.

BASIC COOKIE MIX
from
MAKE-A-MIX COOKERY
by Eliason, Harward & Westover
Published by Bantam
MIXED FOR YOU BY:

BASIC COOKIE MIX makes:
Chocolate Chip Cookies
Very Vanilla Cookies

GRANOLA MIX
from
MAKE-A-MIX COOKERY
by Eliason, Harward & Westover
Published by Bantam
MIXED FOR YOU BY:

GRANOLA MIX makes:
Magic Granola Bars
Breakfast Cookies

CHOCOLATE CHIP COOKIES

Preheat oven to 375°F (190°C). Grease baking sheets. In a large bowl, combine 3 cups BASIC COOKIE MIX, 1 tablespoon milk, 1 teaspoon vanilla and 1 egg. Blend well. Stir in 1/2 cup nuts or coconut and 1 cup chocolate chips or sugar-coated chocolate candies. Drop by teaspoonfuls onto prepared baking sheets. Bake 10 to 15 minutes, until golden brown. Makes about 24 cookies.

VERY VANILLA COOKIES

Preheat oven to 375°F (190°C). Lightly grease baking sheets. In a large bowl, combine 3 cups BASIC COOKIE MIX, 1 teaspoon milk, 1-1/2 teaspoons vanilla and 1 egg. Blend well. Drop by teaspoonfuls onto prepared baking sheets. Sprinkle with sugar, if desired. Bake 10 to 15 minutes, until edges are golden. Frost, if desired. Makes about 24 cookies.

MAGIC GRANOLA BARS

Preheat oven to 350°F (175°C). Put 1/2 cup butter or margarine in a 13″ x 9″ baking pan. Melt in preheating oven. Sprinkle 1-1/2 cups crushed graham crackers evenly over melted butter or margarine. Sprinkle 1-1/3 cups flaked coconut evenly over crumbs. In a small bowl, combine 3/4 cup chocolate chips and 3/4 cup butterscotch chips. Sprinkle over coconut. Sprinkle with 1 cup GRANOLA MIX. Drizzle with 1 (15-oz.) can sweetened condensed milk. Bake about 25 minutes, until chips are melted. Cool. Cut into 2-inch squares. Makes about 24 to 30 squares.

BREAKFAST COOKIES

Preheat oven to 350°F (175°C). Lightly grease baking sheets. Cream together 1/2 cup shortening and 1 cup firmly packed brown sugar in a large bowl. Add 2 eggs, 1 tablespoon milk and 1 teaspoon vanilla. Beat well. In a medium bowl, combine 1-1/4 cups all-purpose flour, 1/2 teaspoon baking soda and 1/4 teaspoon salt. Mix well and add to sugar mixture. Stir in 2 cups GRANOLA MIX. Drop by teaspoonfuls onto prepared baking sheets. Bake 10 to 12 minutes, until edges are browned. Makes about 3 dozen cookies.

MEAT SAUCE MIX
from
MAKE-A-MIX COOKERY
by Eliason, Harward & Westover
Published by Bantam
MIXED FOR YOU BY:

_____

MEAT SAUCE MIX makes:
Speedy Pizza
Rancher's Sloppy Joes

BASIC CAKE MIX
from
MAKE-A-MIX COOKERY
by Eliason, Harward & Westover
Published by Bantam
MIXED FOR YOU BY:

_____

BASIC CAKE MIX makes:
Cherry Dessert Cake
Elegant White Cake

SPEEDY PIZZA

In a small saucepan, simmer 1 pint thawed MEAT SAUCE MIX about 5 minutes, until heated through. Toast 12 English muffin halves. Spoon meat mixture generously over English muffins. Sprinkle with oregano and top each with about 1 tablespoon grated mozzarella cheese. Add pepperoni, mushrooms, green pepper, olives and other toppings, as desired. Broil about 3 to 5 minutes, until cheese is bubbly. Makes 12 individual pizzas.

RANCHER'S SLOPPY JOES

In a medium saucepan, combine 1 pint thawed MEAT SAUCE MIX, 1/4 cup brown sugar, 2 tablespoons vinegar, 1/2 cup ketchup and 1 tablespoon mustard. Cover and cook over medium heat about 10 minutes, until heated through. Serve over hamburger buns. Makes 6 servings.

CHERRY DESSERT CAKE

Preheat oven to 350°F (175°C). Pour 2 (21-oz.) cans cherry pie filling into a 13″ x 9″ pan. Sprinkle 1-1/3 cups BASIC CAKE MIX on top of pie filling. Drizzle 1 cup melted butter or margarine over top of mix. Top with 3 ounces slivered almonds. Bake about 45 minutes, until lightly browned. Cool in pan. Makes 1 large cake.

ELEGANT WHITE CAKE

Preheat oven to 375°F (190°C). Grease two 8-inch, round cake pans. Combine 3-1/3 cups BASIC CAKE MIX and 3/4 cup milk in a large bowl. Beat at medium speed 2 minutes. Scrape bowl and beaters. Add 3 egg whites and 1 teaspoon vanilla. Beat 2 more minutes. Pour into prepared pans. Bake 20 to 25 minutes, until a toothpick inserted in center comes out clean. Cool in pans 10 minutes, then cool on wire racks. Frost as desired. Makes one 2-layer cake, or 24 cupcakes.

CORNMEAL MIX
from
MAKE-A-MIX COOKERY
by Eliason, Harward & Westover
Published by Bantam
MIXED FOR YOU BY:

_____

CORNMEAL MIX makes:
Cornmeal Muffins
Dixie Spoon Bread

GARDEN VEGETABLE MIX
from
MAKE-A-MIX COOKERY
by Eliason, Harward & Westover
Published by Bantam
MIXED FOR YOU BY:

_____

GARDEN VEGETABLE MIX makes:
Alphabet Vegetable Soup
Garden Supper

CORNMEAL MUFFINS

Preheat oven to 425°F (220°C). Butter muffin pans. Put 2-1/2 cups CORNMEAL MIX in a medium bowl. Combine 1 egg and 1-1/4 cups milk in a small bowl. Add all at once to CORNMEAL MIX. Blend. Fill prepared muffin pans 2/3 full. Bake 15 to 20 minutes, until golden brown. Makes 12 large muffins.

DIXIE SPOON BREAD

Preheat oven to 325°F (165°C). Lightly grease a 1-1/2-quart casserole. Scald 2-1/2 cups milk in a small saucepan. Gradually add 2-1/2 cups CORNMEAL MIX, stirring constantly. Continue cooking and stirring until mixture reaches consistency of thick mush. Stir in 2 egg yolks, one at a time. Remove from heat. Stir in 1 cup milk. In a glass bowl, beat egg whites until stiff. Fold into cooked mixture. Put into prepared casserole. Bake about 1 hour, until golden brown. Makes 1 pan of spoon bread.

ALPHABET VEGETABLE SOUP

In a large saucepan, combine 3 cups thawed GARDEN VEGETABLE MIX, 1 quart vegetable juice cocktail, 1/2 teaspoon seasoned pepper and 3/4 teaspoon salt. Bring to a boil. Add 2/3 cups alphabet macaroni and 1 cup pared and cubed potatoes. Reduce heat to medium. Cook uncovered about 12 to 15 minutes, until macaroni and potatoes are tender. Makes 6 to 8 servings.

GARDEN SUPPER

Melt 1/4 cup butter or margarine in a medium saucepan. Sauté 1 chopped medium onion until clear. Add 1/4 cup all-purpose flour and stir to blend well. Add 1-1/2 cups milk. Cook about 3 minutes, stirring constantly, until thick and smooth. Add 1/2 teaspoon salt and 3 cups thawed and drained GARDEN VEGETABLE MIX. Cook uncovered about 5 minutes, stirring occasionally, until vegetables are crisp-tender. Serve over hot cooked rice. Makes 4 to 5 servings.

GINGERBREAD MIX
from
MAKE-A-MIX COOKERY
by Eliason, Harward & Westover
Published by Bantam
MIXED FOR YOU BY:

GINGERBREAD MIX makes:
Snappy Ginger Cookies
Sugar & Spice Gingerbread

WHEAT MIX
from
MAKE-A-MIX COOKERY
by Eliason, Harward & Westover
Published by Bantam
MIXED FOR YOU BY:

WHEAT MIX makes:
Quick Wheat Muffins
Coffeetime Quick Bread

SNAPPY GINGER COOKIES

Preheat oven to 350°F (175°). Lightly grease baking sheets. In a medium bowl, combine 3 cups GINGER-BREAD MIX, 1/3 cup molasses and 1 egg. Blend well. Chill dough for easier handling, if desired. Shape into 1-inch balls. Roll in sugar. Place balls 2 inches apart on prepared baking sheets. Flatten balls with bottom of a small glass. Bake 12 to 15 minutes, until edges are browned. Makes about 24 cookies.

SUGAR & SPICE
GINGERBREAD

Preheat oven to 350°F (175°C). Butter and lightly flour a 9-inch square pan. Combine 1/2 cup milk, 1 egg and 1/2 cup molasses in a medium bowl. Add 2-1/4 cups GINGERBREAD MIX and stir until blended. Pour into prepared pan. Bake about 30 minutes, until a toothpick inserted in center comes out clean. Cool in pan 10 minutes, then cool on a wire rack. Serve with lemon sauce and whipped cream or ice cream, or with fresh sliced bananas or peaches. Makes one 9-inch cake.

QUICK WHEAT MUFFINS

Preheat oven to 400°F (205°C). Generously butter muffin pans. In a medium bowl, combine 3 cups WHEAT MIX and 2 tablespoons sugar. Blend well. Combine 1 slightly beaten egg and 1 cup water in a small bowl. Add all at once to dry ingredients. Stir until just moistened; batter should be lumpy. Fill prepared muffin pans 2/3 full. Bake 15 to 20 minutes, until golden brown. Makes 12 large muffins.

COFFEETIME QUICK BREAD

Preheat oven to 350°F (175°C). Grease a 9" x 5" loaf pan. Combine 1 slightly beaten egg and 1-1/4 cups water in a large bowl. Stir in 4 cups WHEAT MIX until moistened. Turn into prepared pan and bake about 50 minutes, until a toothpick inserted in center comes out clean. Top of loaf should crack. Cool pan on a wire rack about 5 minutes. Loosen sides of bread with a knife and turn right-side up on a wire rack. Cool completely before slicing. Makes 1 loaf.

Spice Chart

NAME AND DESCRIPTION	COMPATIBLE WITH:
Allspice Color—brown Flavor—spicy, sweet, mild, pleasant	All cranberry dishes, spice cakes, beef stew, baked ham, mincemeat and pumpkin pie, tapioca & chocolate pudding
Anise Color—brown with tan stripes Flavor—sweet licorice aroma and taste	Coffee cake, rolls, cookies, all fruit pie fillings, sweet pickles, stewed fruits
Basil Color—light green Flavor—mild, sweet	All tomato dishes, green vegetables, stews, shrimp and lobster dishes
Bay Leaves Color—light green Flavor—very mild, sweet	Vegetables, stews, shrimp, lobster, chicken dishes, pot roasts
Caraway Color—dark brown with light brown stripes Flavor—like rye bread	Cheese spreads, breads and rolls, cookies, vegetables, roast pork
Cardamom Color—cream-colored pod, dark brown seeds Flavor—bitter-sweet	Danish pastry, coffee cake, custards, sweet potato and pumpkin dishes
Cayenne Color—burnt orange Flavor—hot	Deviled eggs, fish dishes, cooked green vegetables, cheese souffles, pork chops, veal stew
Celery Seed Color—shades of brownish green Flavor—bitter celery	Meat loaf, fish chowders, cole slaw, stewed tomatoes, rolls, salad dressings
Chili Powder Color—light to dark red Flavor—distinctive, hot	Mexican cookery, chili, beef, pork and veal dishes, Spanish rice
Cinnamon Color—light brown Flavor—sweet and spicy	Coffee cakes, spice cake, cookies, puddings, fruit pies, spiced beverages, sweet potato and pumpkin dishes
Cloves Color—dark brown Flavor—spicy, sweet, pungent	Ham, apple, mince & pumpkin pies, baked beans, hot tea, spice cake, puddings, cream of pea and tomato soups
Cumin Color—gold with a hint of green Flavor—salty sweet	Deviled eggs, chili, rice, fish

NAME AND DESCRIPTION	COMPATIBLE WITH:

Curry Powder
  Color—Predominantly rich
    gold
  Flavor—exotic with heat
	Eggs, fish, poultry, creamed
	vegetables, chowders, tomato
	soup, salted nuts

Dill
  Color—greenish brown
  Flavor—similar to caraway,
    but milder and sweeter
	Pickling, potato salad, soups,
	vegetables, salad dressing,
	drawn butter for shellfish

Ginger
  Color—tan
  Flavor—spicy
	Cookies, spice cake, pumpkin
	pie, puddings, applesauce,
	stews, French dressing

Mace
  Color—burnt orange
  Flavor—similar to nutmeg,
    exotic
	Fish, stews, pickling, ginger-
	bread, cakes. Welsh rarebit,
	chocolate dishes, fruit pies

Marjoram
  Color—green
  Flavor—delicate
	Lamb chops, roast beef,
	poultry, omelets, stews, stuffings

Mint
  Color—green
  Flavor—sweet
	Jelly, fruit salad, lamb and veal
	roast, tea

Mustard
  Color—light to dark brown
  Flavor—spicy, sharp
	Pickling, Chinese hot sauce,
	cheese sauce, vegetables,
	molasses cookies

Nutmeg
  Color—copper
  Flavor—exotic, sweet
	Doughnuts, eggnog, custards,
	spice cake, coffee cake, pump-
	kin pie, sweet potatoes

Oregano
  Color—green
  Flavor—strong
	Pizza, spaghetti sauce, meat
	sauces, soups, vegetables

Paprika
  Color—red
  Flavor—very mild
	Poultry, goulash, vegetables,
	canapes, chowders

Parsley
  Color—green
  Flavor—mild
	Soups, salads, meat stews, all
	vegetables, potatoes

Pepper
  Color—black or white
  Flavor—spicy, enduring
    aftertaste
	Almost all foods except those
	with sweet flavors. Use white
	pepper when black specks are
	not desired.

Poppy Seeds
  Color—blue-gray
  Flavor—crunchy, nutlike
	Breads and rolls, salad
	dressings, green peas

Rosemary
  Color—green
  Flavor—delicate, sweetish
	Lamb, beef, pork, poultry, soups,
	cheese sauces, potatoes

NAME AND DESCRIPTION	COMPATIBLE WITH:
Saffron Color—red-orange Flavor—exotic	Rice, breads, fish stew, chicken soup, cakes
Savory Color—green Flavor—mild, pleasant	Scrambled eggs, poultry stuffing, hamburgers, fish, tossed salad
Sesame Seeds Color—cream Flavor—crunchy, nutlike	Breads and rolls, cookies, salad dressings, fish, asparagus
Tarragon Color—green Flavor—fresh, pleasant	Marinades of meat poultry, omelets, fish, soups, vegetables
Thyme Color—olive green Flavor—pleasantly penetrating	Tomato dishes, fish chowder, all meats, potatoes
Turmeric Color—orange Flavor—mild, slightly bitter	Pickles, salad dressings, seafood, rice

Metric Chart

CONVERSION TO METRIC MEASURE

WHEN YOU KNOW	SYMBOL	MULTIPLY BY	TO FIND	SYMBOL
teaspoons	tsp	5	milliliters	ml
tablespoons	tbsp	15	milliliters	ml
fluid ounces	fl oz	30	milliliters	ml
cups	c	0.24	liters	l
pints	pt	0.47	liters	l
quarts	qt	0.95	liters	l
ounces	oz	28	grams	g
pounds	lb	0.45	kilograms	kg
Fahrenheit	°F	5/9 (after subtracting 32)	Celsius	C
inches	in	2.54	centimeters	cm
feet	ft	30.5	centimeters	cm

LIQUID MEASURE TO MILLILITERS

1/4 teaspoon	=	1.25 milliliters
1/2 teaspoon	=	2.5 milliliters
3/4 teaspoon	=	3.75 milliliters
1 teaspoon	=	5 milliliters
1-1/4 teaspoons	=	6.25 milliliters
1-1/2 teaspoons	=	7.5 milliliters
1-3/4 teaspoons	=	8.75 milliliters
2 teaspoons	=	10 milliliters
1 tablespoon	=	15 milliliters
2 tablespoons	=	30 milliliters

FAHRENHEIT TO CELSIUS

F	C
200°	93°
225°	107°
250°	121°
275°	135°
300°	149°
325°	163°
350°	177°
375°	191°
400°	205°
425°	218°
450°	232°
475°	246°
500°	260°

LIQUID MEASURE TO LITERS

1/4 cup	=	0.06 liters
1/2 cup	=	0.12 liters
3/4 cup	=	0.18 liters
1 cup	=	0.24 liters
1-1/4 cups	=	0.3 liters
1-1/2 cups	=	0.36 liters
2 cups	=	0.48 liters
2-1/2 cups	=	0.6 liters
3 cups	=	0.72 liters
3-1/2 cups	=	0.84 liters
4 cups	=	0.96 liters
4-1/2	=	1.08 liters
5 cups	=	1.2 liters
5-1/2 cups	=	1.32 liters

INDEX

ABOUT THE AUTHORS

How does someone discover the convenience of Mix Cookery? For NEVADA HARWARD, MADELINE WESTOVER and KARINE ELIASON discovery was the result of their busy schedules. All three lecture, give cooking demonstrations and appear regularly on television in Phoenix, Arizona. All three also maintain homes for large families. Among them they have sixteen children. Several years ago they decided there had to be an easier and quicker way to provide healthful, homemade meals for their families. That's when they discovered the ease and economy of cooking with mixes. Their mixes worked so well, they decided to share their ideas. Together they tested every recipe in this book. Nevada Harward is a graduate of Utah State University where she and Karine Eliason both majored in education. Madeline Westover studied home economics at Brigham Young University. Aside from raising their children, demonstrating cooking techniques and appearing on television, they have created and distributed thousands of information packets containing recipes and home-making hints. They are all active participants in church and civic activities, and their cookbook came out of their efforts to cook for large families while very busy with public lectures and cooking demonstrations. They are involved in the Church of Jesus Christ of the Latter Day Saints and reside with their families in Glendale, Arizona.

KITCHEN POWER!

☐	12207	**COOKING WITH HERBS AND SPICES** Craig Claiborne	$2.50
☐	11371	**SOURDOUGH COOKERY** Rita Davenport	$1.95
☐	10486	**MASTERING MICROWAVE COOKING** Scotts	$1.95
☐	2030	**PUTTING FOOD BY** Hertzberg, Vaughan & Greene	$2.50
☐	2220	**AMERICAN HERITAGE COOKBOOK**	$1.95
☐	11888	**CROCKERY COOKERY** Mable Hoffman	$2.25
☐	8064	**THE COMPLETE BOOK OF PASTA** Jack Denton Scott	$1.25
☐	12241	**MADAME WU'S ART OF CHINESE COOKING**	$1.95
☐	12186	**BETTER HOMES & GARDENS HOME** **CANNING COOKBOOK**	$1.95
☐	10477	**BETTY CROCKER'S COOKBOOK**	$2.25
☐	10538	**AMERICA'S FAVORITE RECIPES FROM** **BETTER HOMES & GARDENS**	$1.50
☐	10539	**BETTER HOMES & GARDENS CASSEROLE COOKBOOK**	$1.50
☐	12309	**THE ART OF FRENCH COOKING** Fernande Garvin	$1.75
☐	12199	**THE ART OF JEWISH COOKING** Jennie Grossinger	$1.95
☐	12316	**THE ART OF ITALIAN COOKING** Mario LoPinto	$1.75

Buy them wherever Bantam Bestsellers are sold or use this handy coupon:

KITCHEN POWER!

☐	11107	**MICHEL GUERARD'S CUISINE MINCEUR** Michel Guerard	$2.50
☐	2708	**COOKING WITHOUT A GRAIN OF SALT** Elma Bagg	$1.95
☐	11782	**ART OF FISH COOKERY** Milo Milorandovich	$1.75
☐	2965	**THE ROMAGNOLIS' TABLE** The Romagnolis	$1.95
☐	6499	**BETTER HOMES & GARDENS COOKING FOR TWO**	$1.25
☐	8809	**THE WORLD-FAMOUS RATNER'S MEATLESS COOKBOOK** Judy Gethers	$1.50
☐	10157	**THE BETTER HOMES & GARDENS BARBECUE BOOK**	$1.50
☐	12215	**THE COMPLETE BOOK OF MEXICAN COOKING** Elisabeth Ortiz	$1.95
☐	10348	**THE FRENCH CHEF COOKBOOK** Julia Child	$2.25
☐	12107	**WHOLE EARTH COOKBOOK** Cadwallader & Ohr	$1.95
☐	10468	**BLEND IT SPLENDID: THE NATURAL FOODS BLENDER BOOK** The Dworkins	$1.50
☐	10532	**BETTER HOMES & GARDENS CALORIE COUNTER'S COOKBOOK**	$1.50
☐	12512	**BETTY CROCKER'S DINNER FOR TWO**	$1.95
☐	11188	**BETTY CROCKER'S DINNER PARTIES**	$1.50
☐	11299	**THE SPANISH COOKBOOK** Barbara Norman	$1.50
☐	11377	**CREPE COOKERY** Mable Hoffman	$1.95